OMISSIONS ARE NOT ACCIDENTS

GENDER
IN THE
ART OF
MARIANNE
MOORE

OMISSIONS
ARE NOT ACCIDENTS

Jeanne Heuving

〰 *Wayne State University Press* Detroit

LIBRARY OF CONGRESS
CATALOGING-IN-PUBLICATION
DATA

Heuving, Jeanne, 1951–
Omissions are not accidents : gender in the art of
Marianne Moore/Jeanne Heuving.
    p.   cm.
    Includes bibliographical references and index.
    ISBN 0-8143-2335-9 (hc : alk. paper)
    1. Moore, Marianne, 1887–1972—Criticism and
Interpretation.
    2. Feminism and literature—United States—His-
tory—20th century.
    3. Women and literature—United States—His-
tory—20th century.
    4. Sex role in literature.   I. Title.
PS3525.05616Z683   1992
811'.52—dc20   92-15343

DESIGNER | S. R. TENENBAUM

COVER ART | S. R. TENENBAUM

PERMISSIONS

CONTENTS

ACKNOWLEDGMENTS

I am indebted to many people for their direct and indirect contributions to this endeavor. For his intellectual guidance and insightful questions in the initial conception and writing stages, I would like to thank Charles Altieri. Carolyn Allen's knowledge of feminist criticism and theory was invaluable to me. Gary Handwerk, Charles Molesworth, and Lisa Steinman provided very useful and thorough criticism on a completed draft of the manuscript. I am also grateful to Charles Molesworth for his generosity in sharing his ideas and resources on Marianne Moore. For other helpful conversations and commentary, I wish to express my gratitude to Tess Gallagher, Claudia Gorbman, Judith Howard, Suzanne Jill Levine, Diane Lichtenstein, Jeffrey Peterson, Belle Randall, Steve Shaviro, and Evan Watkins. I also wish to express appreciation to participants in the Feminist Colloquium at the University of Washington and to Sandra Gilbert and the other members of her seminar on American Sexual Poetics at The School of Criticism and Theory.

It was my pleasure to make the acquaintance of Patricia Willis when I did research on the Marianne Moore Collection at the Rosenbach Museum and Library. Her knowledge and commitment to the study of Marianne Moore enriches the field in numerous ways for all scholars engaged in study of Moore. I also wish to thank Marianne Craig Moore, Literary Executor of the Estate of Marianne Moore, for her permission to quote generously from Moore's unpublished works. The Graduate School Fund of the University of Washington allowed ample quotation of the published works of several poets. Mary Gillis of Wayne State University Press provided thoughtful and excellent editorial assistance. And finally, I wish to express my heartfelt thanks to James Reed who lived with this project from beginning to end and made it a more enjoyable and meaningful venture.

INTRODUCTION

The introduction to a recent volume of critical essays on Marianne Moore describes Moore as an "extraordinary poet-as-poet," whose gender should be of issue "only after the aesthetic achievement is judged as such."[1] In *Omissions Are Not Accidents, Gender in the Art of Marianne Moore,* I argue the opposite: that the aesthetic achievement of Moore's poetry can better be appreciated, and judged, by considering how gender structures her work. Indeed, by attending to Moore's position as a woman within her culture and within language, I have established a comprehensive explanation of the chronological development of her innovative writing.

Feminist literary criticism has been able to discuss the significance of a woman writer's gender to her literary production most propitiously by analyzing its representation of gender and of gender issues. But for women writers, such as Moore, who refuse to make gender a central subject of their writing, this approach offers limited insight. And yet, gender is a crucial determination of Moore's poetic production, and much of her poetry, especially her earlier poetry, can be seen as a creative, and feminist, response to that determination.

Moore's poetry written before 1935 is marked by her paradoxical quest to give expression to a universality and also to herself as a woman. A writer whose work is shaped by beliefs in the transcendence of art, Moore seeks to realize in her poetry many of the effects of a transcendent art. Yet at the same time, she works to modify the pervasive masculine bias that forms much art that has been deemed great. Refusing to write from the position of the "second sex," even to inveigh against her second-rate status, Moore instead produces a

11

poetry which is subversive of existing meanings—a richly ambiguous and multivalent art.

I begin my study with the theoretical assertion that a woman cannot write as a man because of her position in her culture and in language. Central to my development of this idea is Luce Irigaray's critique of the specularity of discourse. Irigaray demonstrates that language systematically reflects men, but does not reflect women. Positioned as the other within language, as the "projective map" that "guarantees the system," women are without a corresponding "projective map" and their subjectivity is therefore problematical.[2] Surely, the tradition of lyric poetry with its dependence on mirroring relations between an "I" and a "you" or an "other" only intensifies this specular bias of language and women's problematic subjectivity. Moore, who claims to call her work "poetry because there is no other category in which to put it," attempts to subvert the specular propensities of lyric poetry and to establish a poetry of her own "self-affection."[3]

The most overreaching commitment of Moore's earlier poetry is her refusal of the forms of hierarchy inherent in a specular writing—of a "heroics" that "confuses transcendence with domination" or an aesthetic in which something is "great because something else is small."[4] And whereas this commitment to non-hierarchical forms of meaning is sometimes expressed in the thematics of Moore's writing, it is carried out most fully in the very forms her writing takes—in quotation of statements from insignificant and anti-poetic sources, in subversion of meanings based on hierarchical dualities, in refusal of singular or climactic resolutions, and in representation of the otherness of others. Indeed, Moore's early use of syllabic verse may well be an effort to give each word and syllable significance apart from structures which unify them—the "rising throbbing curve of emotion" of a more traditional lyric versification.[5]

Moore, who hesitates to criticize publicly her male Modernist peers, nevertheless openly reproves them for their poetic speakers' relations of dominance to the others they depict: the "king, steward, and harper, seated amidships while the jade and the rock crystal course about in solution."[6] But whereas Moore criticizes her male peers for these postures, she also faults female poets for engaging in these same structures of domination, albeit differently. In an essay on Elizabeth Bishop, she observes that "some feminine poets of the present day seem to have grown horns and like to be frightful and dainty by turns; but distorted propriety suggests effeteness." Conversely, Moore commends Bishop for not cutting "into the life of a thing" and for not "degrading" a "garment of rich aesthetic construction . . . to the utilitarian offices of the barnyard."[7]

Moore's remarks on Bishop's poetry are revealing for her own poetry. Refusing to reify existing gender relations through the singular "frightful" or "dainty" stances of a "distorted propriety," Moore rather elects to construct her poetry in such a way that in not degrading "garments of rich aesthetic construction," she does not degrade herself as a woman. Although Moore works to divest her poetry of forms of hierarchy, she also addresses the cultural meanings produced by these hierarchies. Moore's poetry is an ambitious attempt to "change our mortal psycho-structure," while retaining a recognizable cultural basis by which such change is made meaningful.[8]

Moore's reaction against a specular poetics as a woman finds some support in the larger Modernist movement. To a certain extent, the Modernist poetics of many of Moore's male peers, including Eliot, Pound, Williams, and Stevens, can be seen as reactions against a specular writing, in their emphasis on a "direct treatment of the 'thing,' whether subjective or objective," and in their rejection of the vague, abstract, and symbolic languages of nineteenth-century poetry.[9] But there are important differences. Moore's unique psychosexual pressures cause her to work against the strong specular propensities of lyric poetry in a way which is more intensive and extensive. Moore engages the Modernist endeavor of constructing a universal poetics not only refusing but dispossessed of traditional representational conventions. In comparison (as I demonstrate in Chapter 2), her male peers write a kind of erased Romantic lyric.

In examining the chronological development of Moore's poetry, I stress that Moore initially composes a poetry of understatement and later, beginning in the 1930's and 40's, a poetry of overstatement.[10] Indeed, both the earlier and later poetry can be seen as Moore's attempts to mean what she expresses and to express what she means. However, in her earlier poetry, alert to the problematical nature of representational conventions, Moore means far more than she can express; whereas in her later poetry she expresses more than she can mean. Her earlier poetry of understatement enacts Moore's difference from dominant forms of meaning, while her later poetry largely

13

capitulates to them. In her later poetry, Moore no longer attempts the paradoxical quest of writing as a woman and as a universal representative of her culture, as an implied "I", but rather assumes the position of a generalized and far more conventional, implied "we."

The difference between Moore's earlier and later work can be clearly seen in how she expresses her relation to art or to poetry. In her earlier, frequently revised poem, "Poetry," she worries about her own reaction to poetry with respect to its ultimate worth or value, despite its august tradition:

> I, too, dislike it: there are things that are important beyond all
>   this fiddle.
> Reading it, however, with a perfect contempt for it, one
>   discovers in
> it after all, a place for the genuine.

However, in her later "In the Public Garden," Moore assumes both the position and attitude of an undifferentiated public "we," complacently concluding, "Art, admired in general, / is always actually personal."[11] In "Poetry," she inconclusively encounters what is categorized as poetry, writing a memorable and thought-provoking poem; in "In the Public Garden," she finds easy parlance with a commonplace platitude about art.

I trace Moore's poetry of understatement from a poetry of "adverse ideas" (Chapter 3) through a poetry of "agreeing difference" (Chapters 4 and 5).[12] In her poetry of "adverse ideas," Moore's use of singular speakers expressing their views with emotional intensity is well within a traditional lyric mode, but veers from it in her employment of the modes of "contrariety" and the fantastic. "Contrariety" is a term Moore employs early in her career to designate what is for her a desired condition in which both sides of a contention are equally true.[13] In her fantastic poetry, Moore extends her play of meanings— creating uncertainty as to whether the events of her poetry are to be taken as natural or supernatural and whether they are to be read on a literal, allegorical, or symbolic level.[14] Thereafter, rejecting the relative singularity and negativity of the voices of this "adverse" poetry, Moore in her poetry of "agreeing difference" enlists a multiplicity of perspectives, writing many of her most significant poems. In poems based on list and collage formations, Moore directly contests existing expressions and meanings as phrases are played off of one another in a "sea of shifting" "with no weather side."[15]

In concluding with Moore's poetry of overstatement (Chapter 6), I consider the ways in which Moore's later poetry is a falling off from her earlier poetry.[16] Although Moore's earlier poetry can be seen as reacting against the existing specularity of language, it is also a profound, if frustrated, attempt to "see" or to represent herself. Indeed, I suggest, Moore's earlier poetry is far more vital than her later poetry precisely because it is an attempt at self-representation. In her later poetry, Moore no longer engages in her paradoxical quest to construct a universal poetry that includes her perspective as a woman, turning from a subversive poetry marked by ambiguity and multivalency to a far more conventional poetry which evinces considerable thematic and symbolic unity. Indeed, Moore re-enlists many of the hierarchical dualisms carefully undone in her earlier poetry, frequently promoting the conventionally privileged term.

Although in my discussion of Moore I focus primarily on the relation of Moore's gender to her poetic production, an extended analysis of Moore's position within a Protestant, Northeastern, and upper middle class milieu would only strengthen my argument. Surely, Moore's concern with the universal significance of art is highly influenced by those late nineteenth-century, Northeastern, and Protestant processes defined by Ann Douglas as "the feminization of America" and by Alan Trachtenberg as "the incorporation of America," in which an autonomous cultural realm is perceived as a necessary compensation for the excesses of a capitalistic system.[17] In particular, well-off Northeastern Protestant ministers and the female members of their congregations united in the promotion of a non-utilitarian culture of higher learning and of socially meaningful art, without experiencing any compulsion to intervene in or even criticize the market system itself. Thus, was born a "conjunction of culture with wealth and property on one hand, with surrender, self-denial, and subordination to something larger on the other."[18]

While Moore is clearly affected by these trends and ideas, by what Douglas calls "some very imprecisely conceived spiritual values," she also works against their non-material ideology, much as she works against the masculine bias of a so-called universal art.[19] Perhaps the singular most important influence in Moore's life was her mother,

Mary Warner Moore, who as the daughter of a Presbyterian minister and the head of the Moore household, attempted to impress her son and daughter with the spiritual mission to bring enlightenment and culture to others.[20] And while Moore's later poetry largely takes on this mission, Moore's earlier poetry is ambivalent about these cultural commitments. Thus, while throughout her poetic career Moore concerns herself with the permanence and seriousness of art, in her earlier work she also undermines these values. She writes, for example, that art "which would seem to take no caution to be permanent is least ephemeral," and entitles one poem "In This Age of Hard Trying Nonchalance Is Good And."[21]

Moore's well-known election to uphold affirmative rather than negative assertions is most likely attributable to familial, religious, class, and educational influences as well as to her gender. Indeed, Moore's culminating aesthetic of "agreeing difference" enables her simultaneously to assume an expansive and agreeable attitude and to disclose critical differences and discrepancies. Moore can at once approve and disapprove of her culture. Furthermore, by not taking a position with respect to any one attitude or idea, Moore avoids establishing a singular stance and thereby reinscribing unacceptable terms of her culture and of her gender.

In a short story Moore wrote in 1909 when she was a student at Bryn Mawr, Moore creates a female protagonist who as a painter considers her signature. This Miss Duckworth comments to her uncle: "'That is my signature.' A small reddish device lay scrawled against a purple oblong. 'It's an earth worm, rather like one don't you think? Suppose we go?' Her eyes reverted to the worm and a settled gloom appeared to descend upon her."[22] More than two decades later, in 1934, with the approaching publication of her *Selected Poems*, she signs a letter to her brother with her familial nickname "Rat," with the "A" in red and a note "hereinafter called the Author."[23] From her early years at Bryn Mawr through the mid 1930's, Moore is productively uneasy about her subjectivity and authority, creating through innovative writing practices the very possibility of her own self-expression. As a lowly earthworm or as a crafty rat, her poetic consciousness emerges out of the estrangement of a human animal whose keep is decidedly "elsewhere."[24]

1 / "AN ARTIST IN REFUSING"

> What allows us to proceed . . . is that we interpret, at
> each "moment," the *specular make-up* of discourse, that is,
> the self-reflecting . . . organization of the subject in . . .
> discourse. This language work would thus attempt . . . to
> return the masculine to its own language, leaving open
> the possibility of a different language. Which means that
> the masculine would no longer be "everything."
>
> —Luce Irigaray, *This Sex Which Is Not One*[1]

> I read my story yesterday in the proof—I like it fine—It's
> slight as an ice-coated twig but "it is I."
>
> —Marianne Moore, letter to family (1908)[2]

Alongside the high acclaim that Marianne Moore's
poetry has earned, a consistent negative reaction—a reaction of discomfort with the woman herself—has emerged. It would seem that
Moore lacks something—sexuality, womanliness, or courage—and
that this lack has located itself directly in the poetry as restraint,
reticence, humility, self-effacement, sexlessness, emotionlessness,
and powerlessness. Despite frequent claims that Moore is first a
"poet-as-poet," whose gender is decidedly secondary or irrelevant to
her literary achievement, critical response has rarely forgotten that
Moore is indeed a woman.[3] From the early enthusiasm of her Modernist peers to the mixed response of the New Critics and feminist
criticism, Moore's poetry has been faulted repeatedly for its pur-
ported avoidance and suppression of her sexuality and "feminine experience."

Although Ezra Pound praised Moore's poetry highly, he also

remarked that her efforts were marred by her "spinsterly aversion."[4] T. S. Eliot, in a laudatory review focusing on the unusual aspects of Moore's style and technique, concluded, "And there is one final, and 'magnificent' compliment: Miss Moore's poetry is as 'feminine' as Christine Rossetti's, one never forgets that it is written by a woman; but with both one never thinks of this particularly as anything but a positive virtue."[5] Certainly, for Eliot, this almost-a-"positive virtue" is a quiescence in the work, and not an activity.

Beginning with the New Criticism, Moore's stature began to diminish and a more pronounced disapproval of her "suppressed sexuality" emerged. Ironically, while the New Critics would urge an attention to the text, it was at this time that the stereotype of Moore as sexless and neuter became paramount in the criticism.[6] R. P. Blackmur found Moore's poetry to be limited by a sensibility which "imposes limits more profoundly than it liberates poetic energy." He established the cause of this limitation: "There is no sex anywhere in the poetry. No poet has been so chaste."[7] More lugubriously, Randall Jarrell remarked, "We are uncomfortable or else too comfortable—in a world in which feeling, affections, charity are so entirely divorced from sexuality and power, the bonds of the flesh."[8]

Until very recently, feminist criticism of Moore would seem largely to confirm this stereotype.[9] Adrienne Rich denounces Moore as the woman most admired by the men in her generation precisely because her "maidenly," "elegant," and "discreet" qualities posed no threat to her male peers.[10] Suzanne Juhasz, in attempting to see these attributes from Moore's perspective, apologizes for Moore. It seems Moore had to leave out her "feminine experience" "in seeking public recognition at this time," for she had "to play by the boys' rules."[11] Most telling of the pervasiveness of the stereotype of Moore as sexless and passionless is Carolyn Burke's recent revisionary work on Modernist women writers. Posing the question—"What happens when the speaking subject—the 'I' of the poetry—is textually conscious of itself as a producer of language (or as a point of view) rather than a self seeking transcendence or attempting self-celebration"— Burke can only respond negatively to Moore's poetic venture:

> Still, the range of "feminine" virtues seems limited if one's taste runs to subjects other than celebrations of the attentive, imaginative mind's conflict with nature and with the world of artifacts. Possibly the problem lies in Moore's narrow range of feeling, her

18

sense that the "feminine temperament" is or has been circumscribed and therefore must adopt indirection and obliqueness as
forms of limited self-expression. One senses that the obstacles in
the path of this "feminine" temperament outweigh its force and
passion. [12]

In this study, I take direct issue with the stereotype of Marianne
Moore as repressed, sexless, or neuter. Both Moore's poetry and her
position in the culture as a woman are far more complex than this
stereotype indicates. Moore herself isn't so simply reserved, reticent,
or suppressed, but rather practices a reserve in her writing for the
purpose of altering the very meanings she can make. Indeed, as I will
demonstrate, Moore's poetry is an active response to her engendering that enables her to express her will and desire. All of the above
criticism assumes that Moore simply withholds her emotion and sexuality and that her poetry would have more strength and vitality if
she could only find the courage to express herself. Furthermore, it
assumes that in the absence of this expression, Moore may well be
writing a poetry according to the "boys' rules"—a neuter or a neutral
poetry.

I question both of these assumptions by foregrounding the problematical nature of Moore's, or any woman's, self-expression. Indeed,
even if she so wished Moore could not produce a poetry according
to the "boys' rules" (much less a neuter or neutral poetry), for it
would never be received that way. [13] Furthermore, Moore, like any
poet, is not simply expressing her emotion or sexuality, but is engaged in a meaning-making activity that occurs within and through
language and representational conventions which are themselves implicated in and productive of gender differences. Certainly, recent
feminist theory and criticism has shown the problematical nature of
feminine sexuality—and its expression in language and literature—
given the patriarchal or androgynous bias of the larger culture and
its forms of representation. [14] In order to assess Moore's imaginative
activity, then, a critic must first attend to the ways she can "mean"
within her culture—how she can "make meaning"—as different from
the ways that her male Modernist peers can "mean" or "make meaning." [15] For Moore, a practice of reserve in her writing is bound up
both in what she *cannot* and what she *refuses* to say.

For instance, Moore cannot take on a persona such as J. Alfred Prufrock or Hugh Selwyn Mauberly and appear anything but

19

ridiculous. That is, a woman bemoaning her inability to act as a representative figure within her culture is an oxymoron.[16] She can lament aspects of her culture from her position in it as a woman, as a secondary subject, but not as its primary or universal subject. She can speak *about* her culture, but not *as* its representative.

Similarly, Moore cannot portray a significant other with the same meaningful dynamics as a male poet's portrait of her. We have no Modernist Portraits of a Gentleman that fulfill the same function as do the "Portraits of a Lady," or as the myriad representations of women by men in Modernist texts. We might note the improbability of a poem addressed to a male (or even to a female) by a female, which at once elevates him and establishes her dominance over him. She cannot at once elevate him and establish her dominance over him, for by cultural standards he would no longer be a man to be elevated. Men's lyric poetry without an ineffably meaningful female figure as a kind of ideal or sublime would hardly be what it is—and most certainly Romantic and post-Romantic poetry would not be, given its rejection of meanings based on traditional moralities and truths. Frequently, it is the "meaning" of this "other" upon which the poem's coherence, vicissitudes, and closure depend.

Moore's poetry accordingly differs. She cannot assume the position of a masculine "universal" subject, and she cannot depend on the meaningfulness of woman as other. Further, she actively refuses to take on these stances and forms, to write "in drag," as it were.[17] Equally, Moore refuses to make her experience as a woman, as a secondary subject, a direct concern of her poems. Moore—for a variety of reasons—elects not to write a poetry of plaint, of the "blues," of "abandonment."[18] Indeed, she refuses to enact the conditions of her second-rate status, even to complain about them. However, although Moore only very occasionally writes directly *about* women, she does write *as* a woman.[19]

As we shall see, Moore writes a poetry that works against a masculine bias and that manifests her own "self-affection."[20] And because she works against the forms and meanings of existing representational orders, her meanings are rarely conclusive. Moore's notoriously difficult poetry may best be viewed as inconclusive encounters with a literary tradition and larger system of representation which modify and disrupt these orders. The term "encounter" is particularly appropriate for a discussion of Moore's poetry as it suggests its inconclusiveness born out of her engendered difference from the dominant literary tradition and its frequently affiliative and combative postures. Moore, who elected to write a "light essay" on the "futility of introspection" while an undergraduate at Bryn Mawr, produces a poetry of encounters with diction and genre, " 'business documents and school books' " and readers' expectations.[21] Moore's poems as seeming worlds unto themselves often cannot be interpreted through a single heuristic, but mean on many levels at once, and in non-congruent ways.

Throughout this study, I will be emphasizing the ways Moore's "reserve" or "reticence" is a recognition of how an important part of the meanings she can make are unrepresentable. While at times in her critical writing, Moore merely seems to be urging what Gerard Genette calls "plausible" silences and I call articulate silences—the "Pleasure . . . derived from the reader's ability to keep the allegory out of sight"—at other times she suggests that something inarticulate or unrepresentable is at work.[22] Such statements as "one need not know the way / To be arriving," "the avowed artist . . . must be an artist in refusing," "in magnetism the potent factor is reserve," and "omissions are not accidents" suggest that for Moore unreason and unrepresentableness are crucial to meaningful verbal acts.[23] Moore's poetic quest—as I will be developing at some length—is doubly paradoxical: to write a universal poetry which includes her perspective as a woman and to construct a universal consciousness out of a "direct treatment of the 'thing.' "

Pierre Macherey in A Theory of Literary Production and Luce Irigaray in This Sex Which is Not One provide important discussions of how "meanings" in literary texts and other discourses may be unspeakable or unrepresentable. While Macherey and Irigaray differ with respect to the importance they place on an author's or woman's active role in making meaning, both count the ways that literary texts and other discourses disclose and embody that which is unspeakable or unrepresentable as among a text's most significant effects.

For Macherey, the so-called unity or totality of texts is only an illusion, for texts are produced out of incomplete and incompatible meanings, which are socially determined. As products of authors positioned in the culture in certain ways, literary texts—as "free necessities"—emerge out of dissatisfaction with these meanings, although texts do not have the power to complete meanings, but only to "interrogate them." The text, consequently, has no hidden or deep meaning, but rather structures itself around those socially determined contradictions which it cannot resolve. Basing his notion of ideology on Althusser, Macherey does not view history as a "single external relation to the work: it is present in the work in so far as the emergence of the work requires history, which is its only principle of reality and also supplies its means of expression." He adds, "in its every particle the work manifests what it cannot say . . . . This silence gives it life."[24]

Macherey makes the distinction between what an author can't say and refuses to say, but urges that the critic focus on what a text can't say, which is manifested in its paradoxes and contradictions. As do many Marxians, he maintains a concept of authorship as a kind of negative receptivity. The most worthy author is he or she best able to record the paradoxes of his or her time without interfering with these or even extensively analyzing them. A literary artist should aim "to figure" his own historical predicament. Macherey praises Jules Verne as a "true author . . . because he knew how to acquiesce in this decisive interrogation."[25] Attention has been called to the lack of conceptualization of the "acting subject" in Marxian social theories of art, and the Althusserian subject has been criticized as being "empty."[26] While Macherey provides a compelling description of how literary texts emerge out of incomplete and incompatible meanings, he allows writers little capacity to confront these or even to recognize them. Indeed, one wonders if a writer can "decisively acquiesce" in an "interrogation," or if the writer instead actively refuses to make conventionally coherent meanings in the face of irreconcilable social contradictions.

As does Macherey, Irigaray presumes the largely determining aspect of cultural and social languages, although she posits a far more active author or subject. Furthermore, rather than basing her analysis on specific historical periods and dilemmas, she concentrates on how Western discourse since Plato has structured differences between the sexes. For Irigaray, meanings and the act of making meaning are very different for men than for women. Establishing the concept of discourse as a specularity which systematically reflects the masculine as it suppresses the feminine, Irigaray uses, mimics, and disrupts several established discourses in order to reveal her inscription in them as well as her difference from them. For Irigaray, undoubtedly, Macherey's elucidation of literary texts presumes a masculine specular economy in that he can discover himself and his history in the mirror that the literary text offers him as readily as he does.

As a crucial discourse for her exposition, Irigaray uses Lacan's conceptions of the imaginary and symbolic, conflating them in her critique of the specularity of discourse. For Lacan, human identity is a powerful fiction in which the "I," through the mirror of an other or an actual mirror, conceives of himself as total and complete. While the formation of identity as part of Lacan's imaginary is constituted through the "lure of [the] spatial," subjectivity as part of Lacan's symbolic is constituted through language, which is underwritten by the Law of the Father or the Phallus. By acquiring language, the imaginary "I" is deflected into the social "I." However, for the female this deflection does not occur as completely because as a woman she is positioned differently with respect to the symbolic order or the Law of the Father. The female subject remains, at least in part, "excluded by the nature of things which is the nature of words."[27]

Irigaray, then, uses and exploits Lacan's conception of the imaginary and symbolic. For Irigaray, the formation of identity in the mirror stage is implicitly a masculine formation, especially since it can only be conceived retrospectively in language, through the symbolic order underwritten by the Law of the Father. Throughout her writing, Irigaray deliberately conflates the mirror stage with the phallic direction of that identity that occurs through the Law of the Father, emphasizing women's resulting subordination in a specular discourse. And for Irigaray women's position "elsewhere" than this imaginary-symbolic, this specular discourse, is problematical as well as advantageous. It is problematical in that "woman" without her own self-representation is easily absorbed into masculine representations of her—unable to establish the place of her own "self-affection." In his discourse, she remains frozen and mute—a Mirror for him. However, while she is at least partially "excluded by the nature of things which is the nature of words," from Lacan's symbolic, she can experience her difference from his projections of her and from the Law of the Father.

For Irigaray, woman's existence "elsewhere" allows her, then, an important, if partial, freedom from the proper or the symbolic. For

Irigaray, women can begin to speak *as* women in at least two crucial ways. They can mimic the "feminine" as it is prescribed by the "masculine," thereby revealing their difference from this projection. And they can practice a fluid and contradictory writing, a feminine écriture, in which proper meaning is transgressed and subverted. In this writing of her own "self-affection," a woman can disrupt the specularity of discourse by privileging multiplicity over singularity, discontinuity over unity, fluidity over stasis, metonymy over metaphor, comedy over tragedy, openness over closure, and the other as other over the other as mirror.

While feminist literary critics have frequently celebrated how various women's writings form a kind of écriture, Irigaray is far more ambivalent. Concerning women's multiplicity and multiple writing, Irigaray poses the question:

> Must this multiplicity of female desire and female language be understood as shards, scattered remnants of a violated sexuality? A sexuality denied? The question has no simple answer. The rejection, the exclusion of a female imaginary, puts woman in the position of experiencing herself only fragmentarily, in the little-structured margins of a dominant ideology, as waste, or excess, what is left of a mirror invested by the (masculine) "subject" to reflect himself, to copy himself. Moreover, the role of "femininity" is prescribed by this masculine specula(riza)tion and corresponds scarcely at all to women's desire which may be recovered only in secret, in hiding, with anxiety and guilt.

Indeed, for Irigaray there is no final way out of masculine discourse; at best women can only begin "to return the masculine to its own language. . . . Which means that the masculine would no longer be 'everything.'"[28] By Irigaray's account, the female subject is itself a contradiction, a "can't say," existing in an "elsewhere" that has not been absorbed by the self-reflecting, comprehensive systematicity of discourse.

The theoretical writings of Pierre Macherey and Luce Irigaray allow for an elaboration of Moore's doubly paradoxical quest: to write a universal poetry that includes her perspective as a woman and to construct a universal consciousness out of a "direct treatment of the 'thing.'" In both cases, but for different reasons, Moore is working within and against a symbolic or specular form of expression.[29]

As a woman, Moore encounters a poetic tradition which claims to consist of the universal expression of strong speakers when it is in fact structured by a masculine specular economy in which woman as other subtends the representation. Although Irigaray's criticism of the masculine specular nature of meaning addresses all forms of discourse in Western culture, it is particularly relevant to lyric poetry, especially Romantic and post-Romantic poetry, dependent as they are on unspoken assumptions about mirroring relations between an "I" and a "you" or an "I" and an "other."[30] Indeed, I would suggest that an informing convention in the production and reception of poetry up to and including our time, when it is not overtly symbolic, is a specular aesthetic—a sense that the speaker is reflected in some unique way by the poem's representation of that which is outside of or other than the speaker. While certainly many, or all, women poets practice some version of this aesthetic, it is an aesthetic made problematical for a woman by her own figuring as the ultimate other, the "projective map" that "guarantees the system."[31]

Indeed, Moore would seem to be reacting against a specular or symbolic poetry while at the same time employing some of its forms and ideologies. Moore's repeated comments that she does not write poetry, but that she does not know what else to call her work; her disinclination to present singular and powerful speakers; and her presentation of others as others rather than self-reflecting mirrors indicates her felt alienation from the conventions of a traditional lyric poetry. Yet, contradictorily, she will uphold many of the values and effects of a transcendendant art. She asserts, "the secret of burnished writing is strong intention."[32] And while she is compelled by multiplicity, "contradictions," and "tentativeness," she also states that "the final tests" of the imagination are "simplicity, harmony, and truth."[33]

As a writer responsive to the historical and aesthetic tensions that gave rise to the Modernist Movement, Moore, as did her male peers, confronts the contradictions of a poetry that would construct a universal consciousness out of a "direct treatment of the 'thing,' whether subjective or objective." Rejecting the vague, abstract and symbolic languages of the nineteenth-century poetry in favor of a "direct treatment of the 'thing,'" Modernist poets such as Ezra Pound, T. S. Eliot, Wallace Stevens, and William Carlos Williams assumed that a corresponding universal consciousness would simultaneously emerge.

Thus, Eliot in establishing his "objective correlative" at once upholds the writer's unique gift of amalgamating diverse sensory and intellectual experience, while maintaining the universality of the result:

> The only way of expressing emotion in the form of art is by finding an "objective correlative"; in other words, a set of objects, a chain of events which shall be the formula of that particular emotion; such that when the external facts . . . are given the emotion is immediately evoked.[34]

However, Modernist poets failed to understand fully the mediation of language and representational conventions in the "direct treatment of the 'thing.'" While the contradiction between the commitment to a pure seeing and to a universal consciousness is rarely noted by the Modernists themselves, it frequently surfaces in their writings as a problem to be solved. Eliot's "objective correlative," and Pound's concept of Vorticism can be seen as attempts to establish reasons for the universal significance of the arrangement of certain particulars. Moore herself remarks: "When I am as complete as I like to be, I seem unable to get an effect plain enough."[35]

Frederic Jameson in *The Political Unconscious* has pointed to the evolving capitalist economy as the historical cause for what he calls the *rationalization* and *reification* of sense data and consciousness in twentieth-century art. While in Modernist art forms, consciousness and sense data exist in "intimate dialectical relationship," their very separation is part of "a final and extremely specialized phase of that immense process of superstructural transformation whereby the inhabitants of older social formations are culturally and psychologically retrained for life in the market system." That is, like the larger economic system, Modernist art "derealize[s] the content and makes it available for consumption on some purely aesthetic level." Yet, he also stresses that Modernist art

> constitutes a Utopian compensation for everything lost in the process of the development of capitalism—the place of quality in an increasingly quantified world, the place of the archaic and of feeling amid the desacralization of the market system, the place of sheer color and intensity within the grayness of measurable extension and geometrical abstraction.[36]

Jameson's historical analysis in combination with Macherey's textual theory allow for a further articulation of the contradiction in

Modern poetry under discussion. For if, as Macherey maintains, all meanings are born out of social tensions,· out of incomplete and incompatible meanings, one of the major contradictions disclosed by Modern poetry is the way in which the culture detaches its forms of thinking from its referents while thinking through these referents at the same time. That is, if Modern art derealizes content, it also makes that content available for re-presentation, opening up a space for a feminist art or an art of gynesis. [37]

Modernist poetry, in its attempt to "free" the "'thing'" from the abstract languages and symbolism of the preceding century, is itself employed in undoing those "universalizing" languages which would allow it to "mean," while at the same time utilizing these languages. To a certain extent, Modernist poetry itself is a reaction against a specular as well as a symbolic discourse—of a strong speaker's too ready use of an other as a mirror. However, Moore's different psychosexual pressures cause her to work against the symbolic and specular tradition of Romantic and post-Romantic poetry in a way which is both more intensive and extensive than her male peers. Moore, as a Modernist *and* as a woman, confronts the problematic of constructing a universal consciousness dispossessed of as well as refusing traditional representational conventions that would enable her to do so. In comparison, as I shall demonstrate in the next chapter, her male peers write a kind of erased Romantic lyric.

Certainly, Moore's conscious and active participation in the Modernist Movement and its aesthetic concerns is well documented. [38] But in what ways Moore consciously conceived and intended her writing to be different than men's writing is far less apparent. [39] Indeed, although Moore did not make gender an important part of her public identity as a writer, she may have been far less motivated by needs for self-protection than by unwillingness to reinscribe existing gender determinations. She rather elected to address her engendered difference primarily through the subtleness of the poetic medium itself, for as she maintains: "in making works of art, the only legitimate warfare is the inevitable warfare between imagination and medium." [40]

But if Moore did not make her gender an important part of her public identity or a direct concern of most of her poetry, she was openly critical of the overweening presences of her male peers and their presentations of women. She writes negatively of Stevens' "deliberate bearishness—a shadow of acrimonious, unprovoked contumely" and of Williams' "rough and ready girl" in *Paterson*. [41] Of Pound, she criticizes "and apropos of 'feminolatry,' is not the view of woman expressed by the Cantos older-fashioned than that of Siam and Abyssinia?" Furthermore, she reverses the traditional association of women with poetry: "And the Cantos show how troubadours not only sang poems but *were* poems. Usually they were in love, with My Lady Battle if with no other. . . ." [42] In an early piece on William Butler Yeats, she praises Yeats' ease of writing, attributing it indirectly to his gender: "Yeats makes poetry out of the fact that he is a proud, sensitive, cultivated Irishman. He hardly has to make poetry . . . he just lets his heart talk." [43] Later, Moore's attitude toward Yeats is far more negative. Responding to a letter by Elizabeth Bishop in which Bishop expressed her lack of enthusiasm for Yeats, Moore wrote:

> I would be 'much disappointed in you' if you *could* feel about Yeats as some of his acolytes seem to feel. An "effect," an exhaustively great sensibility (with insensibility?) and genius for word-sounds and sentences. But after all, what is this enviable apparatus for if not to change our mortal psycho-structure. [44]

While this response may be seen as a Modernist response to Yeats' neo-Romanticism, it may also be viewed as a feminist reaction, motivated by Yeats' masculine stances and dependence on a specular or symbolic representation of others. Certainly, for Moore, her response as a Modernist and as a woman are inextricably and productively mixed.

Throughout Moore's poetic career, she expressed an uneasiness with self-consciousness. In an early story, "Pym," written while she was an undergraduate at Bryn Mawr, the protagonist, a would-be writer experiences his own point of view as wayward, a problem he vows to correct through an act of mental acquisitiveness: "One must be pertinaciously ingenious as well as genuinely a little blind, to follow long a course which insists upon maintaining its original experimental character. . . . I shall go in for some kind of experience and repair to grow mentally acquisitive. I am all too conscious of my having a 'point of view.'" [45] And in "Feeling and Precision," Moore notes, "Voltaire objected to those who said in enigma what others had said naturally and we agree; yet we must have the courage of our peculiarities."[46] However, to conceive of Moore's uneasiness in any simplistic way, as a discomfort with an actual "self," is to discount the contradictions which structure Moore's efforts as a woman and poet—her very real problems with "self"-expression. Indeed, by Irigaray's account, Moore, or any woman writer, can never "truly" express herself, and certainly not within a lyric tradition highly dependent on specular and symbolic forms of representation. In other words, given the cultural languages and representational forms available to Moore, she can neither embrace nor divorce herself from "sexuality and power, the bonds of the flesh."[47]

MOORE'S "HIGH" MODERNISM:

A Comparison with Her Male Peers

> Some feminine poets of the present day seem to have
> grown horns and to like to be frightful and dainty by
> turns; but distorted propriety suggests effeteness.
>
> —Marianne Moore, *Trial Balances* (1935)[1]

> In making works of art, the only legitimate warfare is the
> inevitable warfare between imagination and medium. . . .
>
> —Marianne Moore, *The Dial* (1926)[2]

Before beginning my discussion of the chronologi-
cal development of Moore's poetry, I shall substantiate and augment
my foregoing claims by comparing specific poems by Moore with
poems by Eliot, Pound, and Williams. I maintain that to some extent
all of the Modernist poets are reacting against a symbolic or specular
aesthetic, but that Moore's reaction is far more intensive and extensive. In comparison to Moore, her male peers write a kind of erased
Romantic lyric—a poetry underwritten by the convention of powerful speakers establishing their authority and identity through mirroring others.

In order to examine how Moore's poetry differs from the poetry
of her male peers, I first consider poems in which the address of an
"I" to a "you" forms the dominant rhetorical situation: Eliot's "Portrait
of a Lady," Pound's "Portrait d'une Femme," Williams' "Portrait of a
Lady," and Moore's "Those Various Scalpels." While the speakers in
the men's poems encounter difficulties establishing their identities
through their relationship to their less than ideal "ladies" and
"femmes," the dynamics of their poems depend on the presumption

of and search for these connections. Moore's speaker, on the other hand, remains outside this dynamic, disclosing and questioning the conventions upon which traditional love lyrics depend.

I then compare poems in which meditations by a singular consciousness on his or her culture provide the major poetic drama: Eliot's "The Love Song of J. Alfred Prufrock," Pound's "Hugh Selwyn Mauberly," and Moore's "No Swan So Fine." All three poems are at least partially elegiac with respect to an earlier culture, and all register a sense of irrevocable change. However, although the speakers in "Prufrock" and "Mauberly" can't fully establish their identities through their representation of cultural others, they presume and seek out the possibility of such specularity. In contrast, Moore's non-personified and de-centered speaker seems to offer only a simple description, moving through and across contradictory visions.

In attempting to write as both a universal representative and as a woman, Moore works against the masculine bias of the medium itself. Moore's speakers are not concerned with constructing an identity through others, but rather with encountering the otherness of others. Although Moore's unpossessive relationship to the others of her poems has been commented on by several prominent critics, it has not been linked to her position within the larger culture as a woman, but rather viewed as a moral, temperamental, or aesthetic disposition. By viewing this "predilection" of Moore's verse as simply due to her disposition, critical response to the poetry has tended to confirm the stereotype of Moore as removed and pristine, rather than as a poet who actively creates the conditions of her creativity. Bonnie Costello, for example, in making Moore's phrase "imaginary possessor" into an epithet for her entire work, *Imaginary Possessions*, also comments that Moore "lack[s] a grasp of her world."[3] Hugh Kenner, in noting that "at [Moore's] best, she was other from us, and her subjects other from her," aestheticizes Moore along with her poetry.[4]

Indeed, in composing "Those Various Scalpels," Moore may have been responding fairly directly to Pound's and Eliot's "Portraits," published a short time before.[5] In a review of Eliot's *Prufrock and Other Observations*, she singles out "Portrait of a Lady" for its "youthful cruelty," referring uneasily to herself as "this hardened reviewer":

The gentle reader, in his eagerness for the customary bit of sweets, can be trusted to overlook the ungallantry, the youthful

31

cruelty, of the substance of the "Portrait." It may as well be admitted that this hardened reviewer cursed the poet in his mind for this cruelty while reading the poem; and just when he was ready to find extenuating circumstances—the usual excuses about realism—out came this "drunken helot" . . . with that ending. It is hard to get over this ending with a few moments of thought; it wrenches a piece of life at the roots.[6]

Although Moore does not elaborate on how Eliot's ending "wrenches a piece of life at the roots," her own poem provides an implicit and powerful criticism of Eliot's "Portrait," and other poems like it.

In the "Portraits" of Eliot, Pound, and Williams, the male speaker establishes himself as superior to the woman he addresses. Although the meanings in these poems are far more complex than these acts of simple domination, by using a female figure as a mirror or foil, the male speaker can construct an authoritative stance from which to write, as well as establish his own relative superiority and wholeness. In all of these poems, the women are characterized by their bodily parts or partial nature: Pound's "oddments," Eliot's "bric-a-brac," and Williams' "petals from an apple tree." In her essay, "Diana Described: Scattered Women and Scattered Rhyme," Nancy Vickers analyzes a specific kind of specular poetry—the Renaissance convention of the portrayal of the beloved through a depiction of her bodily parts. Vickers maintains that this scattering of her parts is actually a projection of the male speaker's own scattered parts, his fear of castration. By projecting his scattered parts onto a female other, the male speaker can convince himself of his wholeness: "it is in fact, the loss at a fictional level of Laura's body [in Petrarch's sonnets] that constitutes the intolerable absence. . . . 'Woman remains the instrument by which man attains unity and she pays for it at the price of her own dispersion.'"[7]

Although Moore, too, in "Those Various Scalpels," employs this Renaissance convention, her speaker remains outside of its specular psychology. Furthermore, she registers the problematic of such a practice—"surgery is not tentative"—and concludes her poem with a critique of the conventions of the love lyric itself: "Why dissect destiny with instruments which / are more highly specialized then the tissues of destiny itself?" Both Pound's and Eliot's poems were written relatively early in their careers—at a time during which they were far more aware of what they were refusing in the poetic tradition than of what they would contribute—and appropriately their ladies are presented as considerably older than they and convey a corrupt moodiness. In neither poem does the speaker profess love for his lady, using her far more flagrantly than does Petrarch in his sonnets as an idealizing mirror in which to reflect himself. Indeed, in these poems of uncertain desire and self-preoccupation, the specular conventions of lyric poetry are far more egregious and may account for the guilt that haunts Eliot's poem.

In Pound's "Portrait d'une Femme," the partial and secondary nature of this "femme" made of parts is openly declared:

> Your mind and you are our Sargasso Sea.
> London has swept about you this score years
> And bright ships left you this or that in fee:
> Ideas, old gossip, oddments of all things,
> Strange spars of knowledge and dimmed wares of price.
> Great minds have sought you—lacking someone else.
> You have been second always. Tragical?
> No. You preferred it to the usual thing;
> One dull man, dulling and uxorious
> One average mind—with one thought less each year. [8]

While this femme is unequivocally secondary to the "great minds" which have sought her—"lacking someone else"—she is respected for electing this life over companionship with "one dull man." As one of her visitors, the speaker assumes the status of one of the "great minds" who visit her, and is certainly not a "dulling and uxorious" houseboy. Intrigued by the "strange gain" the woman offers ("the fiction" she makes possible), he notes that nothing she herself possesses—no "strange spar of knowledge"—is itself "useful." The poem concludes with the femme's interchanging presence and absence—her light and dark—and the speaker's unremitting naming of her:

> and yet
> For all this sea-hoard of deciduous things.
> Strange woods half sodden, and new brighter stuff:
> In the slow float of differing light and deep,
> No! there is nothing! In the whole and all,
> Nothing that's quite your own.
> Yet this is you.

Pound's speaker may not be projecting his bodily parts onto his beloved, but his femme is certainly a projection of partial and somewhat worthless knowledges. And while the problem of establishing a
whole out of discrete parts is of utmost concern to Pound at this
point in his career, he experiences a small "gain" through his authoritative speaker's relation to this femme. In comparison to this lady,
the speaker is in much greater command of the whole of knowledge
and of whole knowledges.

In Eliot's "Portrait," the speaker's relationship to his lady is more
uncertain and dynamic than in Pound's poem. But even though he is
unsure of himself, he and his lady conspire to construct his superiority:

> She has a bowl of lilacs in her room
> And twists one in her fingers while she talks.
> 'Ah, my friend, you do not know, you do not know
> What life is, you who hold it in your hands';
> (Slowly twisting the lilac stalks)
> 'You let it flow from you, you let it flow,
> And youth is cruel, and has no remorse
> And smiles at situations which it cannot see.'
> I smile, of course,
> And go on drinking tea. [9]

Even though her life among the "bric-a-brac" is "composed . . . so
much of odds and ends," she manages to compose the scene for him:

> Among the smoke and fog of a December afternoon
> You have the scene arrange itself—as it will seem to do—
> With 'I have saved this afternoon for you'

While the lady seems to represent some kind of music, or state of
desire—perhaps Eliot's dislike of what he perceived as "feminine"
vagueness and moodiness found in turn-of-the century poetry or in
women themselves—he has little surety with which to oppose her
music, and questions himself:

> I keep my countenance,
> I remain self-possessed
> Except when a street piano, mechanical and tired

34

Reiterates some worn-out common song
With the smell of hyacinths across the garden
Recalling things that other people have desired
Are these ideas right or wrong?

The lady's suggestion that he write to her causes his self- possession
to "gutter."

'Perhaps you can write to me.'
My self-possession flares up for a second;
This is as I had reckoned.
'I have been wondering frequently of late
(But our beginnings never know our ends!)
Why we have not developed into friends.'
I feel like one who smiles, and turning shall remark
Suddenly, his expression in a glass
My self-possession gutters; we are really in the dark.

Why the speaker elects to visit this lady who, about "to reach her
journey's end," causes him such discomfort and even guilt, is not entirely clear. In her presence, the speaker would seem, in Eliot's own
critical vocabulary, to experience an emotion "in excess of the facts
as they appear."[10] However, even though the speaker questions his
own superiority and loses his composure, the very possibility of his
dominance creates the dynamics and the basic conditions of meaning in the poem. Although the poem concludes with the speaker's
wondering whether this woman has the "advantage after all," in the
very last line he asserts the possibility of his own superiority: "And
should I have the right to smile?" For Moore, of course, it was this
last line that clinched her own opinion about the poem: "it wrenches
a piece of life at the roots."

In Williams' "Portrait of a Lady," the speaker reaches a more decisive crisis than in Eliot's poem, and achieves a greater resolution. Unlike in Pound's and Eliot's poems, the speaker desires his lady physi-
cally:

Your thighs are appletrees
whose blossoms touch the sky.
Which sky? The sky
where Watteau hung a lady's

slipper. Your knees
are a southern breeze—or
a gust of snow. Agh! what
sort of a man was Fragonard?
—as if that answered
anything. Ah, yes—below
the knees, since the tune
drops that way, it is
one of those white summer days,
the tall grass of your ankles
flickers upon the shore—
Which shore?—
the sand clings to my lips—
Which shore?
Agh, petals maybe. How
should I know?
Which shore? Which shore?
I said petals from an appletree. [11]

While in his description of this lady, the speaker manages virtually
to enact her disappearance in the largeness of her outlandish parts,
the word "shore" interrupts his revery, focusing his anxiety. Although
the "shore" he imagines initially may be the sea shore (and his lady
by association Venus), or it may be the "shore" between the lady's
legs, the word brings up the possibility of a cutting or tearing, re-
minding him of smaller, more discrete parts: "Which shore? Agh,
petals maybe." In rapidly questioning himself, "Which shore? Which
shore?" the possibility surfaces that the speaker might shore himself
up through another's shoring. In the last line, he projects the multiple
shorings away from himself and onto the lady whose thighs were
initially compared to appletrees: "I said petals from an appletree."
The speaker asserts his dominance over the parts, for it is he who
names them.

In "Those Various Scalpels," Moore too portrays the beloved
through the depiction of bodily parts, but her speaker does not assume a relationship of superiority or of dominance over the other
she depicts. Nor is the speaker primarily concerned with establishing
her own identity with respect to this other. The entity itself, its
"raised hand / an ambiguous signature," is highly indeterminate. It is

unclear, for instance, whether it is male or female, subject or object, fearful or fearsome, a wielder of scalpels or the victim of weapons.[12] In addition, Moore subverts a number of language practices on which intelligible discourse depends, breaking down hierarchies and distinctions between figurative and literal, metaphor and metonymy, figure and ground, and opinion and description. (Although arguably, Moore's male peers subvert language in similar ways, Moore does so to a far greater extent, as will be made evident from my discussion of "Those Various Scalpels.") And while Moore carefully (and lovingly) employs the Renaissance convention of the portrayal of the beloved through the depiction of her bodily parts, she also criticizes this convention.

The poem's title "Those Various Scalpels" serves as a lead into the poem:

> Those
> various sounds consistently indistinct, like intermingled
>   echoes
>   struck from thin glasses successively at random—the
>   inflection disguised: your hair, the tails of two fighting-
>   cocks head to head in stone—like sculptured
>   scimitars re-
>   peating the curve of your ears in reverse order: your eyes,
>   flowers of ice
>
> and
> snow sown by tearing winds on the cordage of disabled ships:
>   your raised hand
>   an ambiguous signature: your cheeks, those rosettes
>   of blood on the stone floors of French chateaux, with regard
>   to which the guides are so affirmative:
>   your other hand
> a
> bundle of lances all alike, partly hid by emeralds from Persia
>   and the fractional magnificence of Florentine
>   goldwork—a collection of half a dozen little objects made
>   fine
>   with enamel in gray, yellow, and dragon fly blue; a lemon,
>   a

pear
and three bunches of grapes, tied with silver: your dress, a
    magnificent square
cathedral of uniform
and at the same time, diverse appearance—a species of
    vertical vineyard rustling in the storm
of conventional opinion. Are they weapons or scalpels?
  Whetted

to
brilliance by the hard majesty of that sophistication which
    is su-
perior to opportunity: these things are rich
instruments with which to experiment but surgery is not
    tentative. Why dissect destiny with instruments which
  are more highly specialized than the tissues of destiny
    itself?

Ultimately, Moore is encountering and interpenetrating two figures in this poem: the entity itself, and the poetic figure which cuts the body into parts. While Moore questions a method in which destiny is dissected by "instruments which / are more highly specialized than the tissues / of destiny itself," to write her poem at all she has had to employ a method of dissection. Moore's brilliance in the poem is that the figure is not merely depicted by bodily parts, but by the depictions that depict it. By making us aware of a "surgery" that "is / not tentative," the tearing and blood presented by the imagery seem the effect of the incision of the metaphors themselves.

In this poem, Moore would seem to want to have it both ways— to use those language conventions which articulate, as well as break up, destiny and to reject those language conventions. In order to portray her entity, whose "destiny" may be occluded because it is articulated through his scalpels ("are they weapons?"), but would equally be occluded without the articulations of language, Moore's only choice may be to refuse to choose and to deploy her language a little differently. By literalizing the effects of these metaphors in images of tearing and blood, Moore instates the relatively literal within the relatively figurative.

Margaret Homans in *Bearing the Language* theorizes women writers' different relationship to the literal and figurative (symbolic) registers. Homans suggests that women writers may be more compelled by the relatively literal than the relatively figurative for a series of complex and contradictory reasons, which I will only highlight. Alienated from Lacan's symbolic or a figurative language, women may be attracted to the non-symbolic, since the "meaning" of the symbolic for women is often their own silence and objectification. Furthermore, women writers may wish to reproduce the experience of mothering in "bearing the word"—in making "real"—the merely conceived, the merely figurative. However, as Homans points out, a woman's alignment with the "real" or the "literal" is itself problematic. Indeed, from the perspective of an androcentric culture and literary tradition, in associating herself with the real, a woman writer is establishing her place with "the silent object of representation, the dead mother, the absent referent, so that within a literary text the shift from figurative to literal connotes a shift from the place of the signifier, the place of the speaking subject to the place of the absent object."

Of the several different textual moments that Homans establishes as instances of women writers "bearing the word," two are especially relevant to Moore's poetry: moments in which overtly figurative language is literalized into an actual event or circumstance and moments when texts reproduce through translation, transmission, or copying the words of other texts. "Those Various Scalpels" provides a preeminent example of the former, and Moore's use of quotations in general provides a marked example of the latter. Furthermore, her use of syllabics and of seemingly arbitrary line breaks, her refusal "to imitate the rising throbbing curve of emotion," suggests that she wishes to maximize attention to *all* parts of her poetry, to the literal, material manifestation of her writing. [13] While these practices may be viewed through a Chodorowian perspective (which Homans favors), as a reproduction of the literal mother, of mothering—a provocative thesis especially for Moore, given her artistic collaboration with her mother—they may also be seen from the perspective of Irigaray's theories as a subversion of a specular/symbolic discourse. [14]

In "Those Various Scalpels," then, Moore performs a number of "war-like" actions on the medium. While the poem seems to be organized through a recounting of bodily parts and metaphors, the metaphors themselves develop metonymically, as if possessed of a life of their own. In an early essay on Moore, T. S. Eliot describes the rhythm of the poem as depending upon "the transformation-changes from one image to another, so that the second image is superposed before the first has quite faded."[15] In his example of "your eyes" as "flowers of ice / And snow sown by tearing winds on the cordage of disabled ships," the initial metaphors proceed through metonymic connections to tell the story of a disabled ship. Likewise, "your dress" proceeds from "a magnificent square / cathedral of uniform and at the same time diverse appearance" to "a species of / vertical vineyard rustling in the storm / of conventional opinion."

In addition to subverting the conventional hierarchy between figurative and literal, and metaphor and metonymy, the poem subverts hierarchies between opinion and description, and figure and ground. Description metamorphoses into opinion in a seamless poetic web: "those rosettes / of blood on the stone floors of French chateaux, with regard to which the guides are so / affirmative." Furthermore, ground and figure are deliberately mixed, "successively at random." While the majority of the poem consists of an elaboration of the entity's parts and of a concluding meditation on the incisions that have transpired, the poem begins with a seemingly unrelated meditation on "Those / various sounds." While these may be the sounds of the footsteps on the stone floor of the French chateaux mentioned later in the poem, the internal sounds that Moore hears and that motivate the writing of this poem, or the language/scalpels of the indeterminate entity's communications, they are transcribed as if they are simply another bodily part.

In comparison to the men's "Portraits," Moore's "Those Various Scalpels" is far more complex and unresolved, disclosing an ambiguous and multivalent world. When "Those Various Scalpels" was published in Moore's first volume of poems, Mark Van Doren commented in a review that it was "fastidiously" "highbrow."[16] However, while it cannot, and refuses, to convey a recognizable masculine psychology, this poem is replete with the "bonds of the flesh"[17]—a bondage that extends into the tissues of language and destiny itself. What Moore refuses in this poem is to portray an other in order to reflect herself. And she equally refuses to assume a position of secondariness in order to presume an advocacy for the other that would only enact those subject-object distinctions through and by which domination occurs. Indeed, Moore would seem to wish to instate the figure of the other as other, marked quite literally by those language conventions that articulate it in all its complexity and retrogressive pain as the singular subject of her poem.

In Eliot's "The Love Song of J. Alfred Prufrock," Pound's "Hugh Selwyn Mauberly," and Moore's "No Swan So Fine," the poetic speakers retain the same relation to others and otherness as in the poets' previous poems. However, in these poems the others are the visual and verbal embodiment of a culture which is passing and changing. Indeed, Prufrock and Mauberly address the problem of identity in a culture which no longer reflects them. But whereas in the "Portraits" the male speakers establish at least a provisional identity through their others, their femmes and ladies, in these later poems their own centrality in a culture with which they are out of step haunts them in the spectre of men they would rather not be. Although they blame the age's "tawdry cheapness" and "one night cheap hotels," they also intimate social and psychological changes to which they cannot adequately respond. They cannot "forge Achaia" or even "force the moment to its crisis." Conversely, in Moore's "No Swan So Fine," her speaker, who does not seek to be reflected by the larger culture, is able both to mourn the passing culture represented by the "still waters of Versailles" and to celebrate the new order in her vision of the swan at the end of the poem: "at ease and tall. The king is dead." Indeed, by concluding her poem with the celebratory "The king is dead," Moore establishes a historical cause for her non-specular seeing and for the "elsewhere" of her vision.

Much of the characterization of Modernism is, in fact, taken from Eliot's and Pound's anguished personae in these poems, and feminist critics such as Shari Benstock have been quick to point out how a description of Modernism which emphasizes "'despair, hopelessness, paralysis, angst, and a sense of meaninglessness, chaos, and fragmentations of material reality' excludes—for a variety of reasons—many women Modernists."[18] While Benstock and other critics urge a consideration of the different experiences and realities of men and women in the twentieth century, I stress the impossibility of a woman's speaking *as* a universal representative of her culture and the inherent absurdity of a woman's foundering identity amidst passing cultural values that exclude and devalue her. In "No Swan So Fine," Moore addresses the paradox of writing a universal poetry that includes her perspective as a woman by positing her de-centered seeings, if not her person, as representative. No central subject, no internal king, haunts her poem with its "maudlin confession," or its "hundred indecisions" and "hundred visions and revisions," looking for its reflection in an other.

Although I am contrasting Eliot's and Pound's poems to Moore's with respect to their more centrally posited speakers who seek to establish their identities through specular and symbolic relations to cultural forms of representation, their poems are frequently contrasted to the poems of the preceding century in much these same terms. As I establish in the previous chapter, the Modernist movement itself can be seen as a rejection of an easy symbolism or specularity present in nineteenth-century poetry. In fact, Eliot's and Pound's search for cultural mirrors is most likely intensified by an aesthetic that makes specularity problematical. However, in comparison to Moore, their poetry is much more concerned with searching for mirrors by which to construct and reflect their identities.

Certainly, in poems such as *The Wasteland* and in many of *The Cantos*, Pound and Eliot reject the more singular consciousness of a Prufrock or a Mauberly. However, a central consciousness seeking its reflection continues to dominate in these poems far more than in Moore's. Eliot's attitude of disgust in *The Wasteland* as well as in *The Four Quartets* is a product of a consciousness in opposition to a culture which does not provide it ideal mirrors. Likewise, in *The Cantos*, Pound initially establishes his authority through the cadences of a relatively unknown Latin translator of Homer's *Odyssey*, Andreas Divus. Making the transition from the earlier "Ur" Cantos, with their disgruntled description of poetry as a "rag bag to stuff all thoughts in," to the rich, resolved cadences of his first completed Canto, Pound writes,

> "Not by the eagles only was Rome measured"
> "Wherever the Roman speech was, there was Rome."
> Wherever the speech crept, there was mastery
> Spoke with the law's voice . . .
>   . . . . Doughty's "divine Homeros"
> Came before sophistry. Justinopolitan
> Uncatalogued Andreas Divus,
> Gave him in Latin, 1538 in my edition, the rest uncertain,
> Caught up his cadence word and syllable:
> "Down to the ships we went, set mast and sail . . ."

"And then went down to their ship, set keep to breakers,
Forth on the godly sea. . . ."[19]

By identifying himself with an earlier Latin translator of Homer,
Pound can establish his authority as part of an ancient and ongoing
"cultural law." Unlike Moore's borrowings of other people's expressions—her "bearing" as well as ironizing the word—Pound's emphasis is on his identification with the translator and on the "mastery" of
Roman speech.

In "Prufrock" and "Mauberly," the speakers' frustrated quests to locate self-reflecting mirrors in the cultural detritus called up by the
poems is heightened in these poems' conclusions. Both Eliot and
Pound stop their speakers' unhappy, proliferating meditations by
making the "I"'s drown or disappear, and concluding their poems with
women who are completely other. Indeed these specular quests come
to an untoward end in their very inversion: the "I"'s are vanquished
and the unreflecting mirrors remain. Throughout his love song, J.
Alfred Prufrock is haunted by a number of different women who
"come and go," with whom he either doesn't want to or can't quite
connect. However, at the end of the poem, he encounters mermaids
who, while decidedly other from him, have the power to disrupt his
solipsistic meditation:

I have heard the mermaids singing, each to each.

I do not think that they will sing to me.

I have seen them riding seaward on the waves
Combing the white hair of the waves blown back
When the wind blows the water white and black.

We have lingered in the chambers of the sea
By sea-girls wreathed with seaweed red and brown
Till human voices wake us, and we drown. [20]

While initially Prufrock assumes that the mermaids will not sing for
him, in the last stanza he suddenly imputes that perhaps "we"—
presumably the poem's initial "you and I"—have been with the mermaids all along. By associating his poem's "etherized" and etherealiz-
ing consciousness with this otherness, Eliot positions Prufrock in an

oppositional relationship to the "human voices" that have the capacity to wake "us" into drowning. Although previously in the poem Prufrock was the representative human voice—if an anti-heroic one—now he has flip-flopped. Refusing to suffer his "human" consciousness any longer, Prufrock, himself now an "other" or an "it," cannot save itself. And although drowning is hardly a positive conclusion, it does bring to an end Prufrock's estranged consciousness and allows Eliot to conclude his poem. That Eliot elects to close his poem by drowning its consciousness attests to his failed attempt to position this consciousness with respect to a cultural other in any empowering way.

In "Hugh Selwyn Mauberly," Pound recounts the misadventures of a male artist, presumably modeled after himself at an earlier stage in his life. While Pound in his disjunctive shifting between a first person and third person perspective creates a far less singular consciousness than does Eliot in "Prufrock," he, like Eliot, stages the drowning (or disappearance) of his protagonist. In the penultimate section of "Mauberly," Pound portrays a physical sensuality so replete that articulation is virtually impossible. As in Eliot's poem, the "I" abnegates its quest to mirror itself in an other by positing an absolute other—in "Mauberly," a nature of such "thick foliage" that it blots out the "I":

> Scattered Moluccas
> Not knowing, day to day,
> The first day's end, in the next noon;
> The placid water
> Unbroken by the Simoon;
>
> Thick foliage
> Placid beneath warm suns,
> Tawny fore-shores
> Washed in the cobalt of oblivions;
>
> Or through dawn-mist
> The grey and rose
> Of the juridical
> Flamingoes;
>
> A consciousness disjunct,
> Being but this overblotted

Series
Of intermittences;

Coracle of Pacific voyages,
The unforecasted beach;
Then on an oar
Read this:

"I was
And I no more exist;
Here drifted
An hedonist."

Pound concludes "Mauberly" with a reality quite other than Mauberly himself, but one finally in which the "I" feels the necessity of leaving some reminder or remnant of himself. His words, once possessed of an initiating authority, are now only to be found inscribed on a wooden oar within quotation marks.

The poem ends with a postscript to this postscript, the "Medallion"—an image of Anadyomene (a Venus figure bearing an uncanny physical likeness to Moore) whose intractable polish provides a mirror too hard and luminous for Mauberly's or Pound's self-reflection. As does Eliot, Pound concludes his poem by establishing Mauberly's powerlessness. Indeed Anadyomene's eyes seem to fix Mauberly/Pound in their gaze, turning a sultry "topaz" in their sexual superiority.

The sleek head emerges
From the gold-yellow frock
As Anadyomene in the opening
Pages of Reinach.

Honey-red, closing the face-oval,
A basket-work of braids which seems as if they were
Spun in King Minos' hall
From metal, or intractable amber;

The face-oval beneath the glaze,
Bright in its suave bounding-line, as,
Beneath half-watt rays,
The eyes turn topaz.[21]

In Moore's "No Swan So Fine," there is no central speaker who experiences diminishment or aggrandizement because she is or is not reflected by her culture or by its others. Of her china swan Moore has no cause to remark, as does Pound in "Mauberly," "The glow of porcelain / Brought no reforming sense / To his perception / Of the social inconsequence," since for Moore consciousness and the objects of her contemplation neither oppose nor reflect each other.[22] Indeed, "No Swan So Fine" focuses on those social and power relations which determine consciousness and being. The "gondoliering" swan in the first stanza who wears a collar "to show whose bird it was" is replaced by the swan in the second stanza which "perches," "at ease and tall," now that the "king is dead."[23] Certainly, one of the achievements of the poem is the way it moves so assuredly and convincingly from an elegiac vision of a passing Versailles, to a mournful and somewhat comic depiction of a captive swan, and then to a healthful and life-giving embodiment of a swan in a "kingless" country:

> "No water so still as the
>   dead fountains of Versailles." No swan,
> with swart blind look askance
> and gondoliering legs, so fine
>   as the chintz china one with fawn-
> brown eyes and toothed gold
> collar on to show whose bird it was.
>
> Lodged in the Louis Fifteenth
>   candelabrum-tree of cockscomb
> tinted buttons, dahlias,
> sea-urchins, and everlastings,
>   it perches on the branching foam
> of polished sculptured
> flowers—at ease and tall. The king is dead.

How Moore invokes three very different visions in such a short poem is remarkable. While the speaker's stance of moving through and across visions without worrying about her identification or lack of identification with them allows for this change, it is achieved by delicate shifts in imagery and language which maintain similarities while interjecting differences. The initial, distilled vision of absence and dying brought forth in "'No water so still as the / dead fountains of Versailles'" is replicated in the vision of the swan, only the vision is of a less absolute absence and death. As part of the passing elegance of Versailles, the swan is to be mourned, but, as a bird who wears a "toothed gold / collar on to show whose bird it was," it also seems mournful. By replicating her syntax, "No Swan So Fine," "'No water so still . . .'" and "No swan . . . so fine," Moore reproduces the mirroring effects of the still waters, intoning the swan with the same majesty with which she refers to Versailles. However, by shifting her vision from something to be mourned to something that is itself mournful, she introduces a slight note of comedy into this tragic scene. The sound relations of soft consonants and open vowels convey aurally the swan's limp and pathetic "look askance" and "gondoliering legs." Yet the effect is also one of opening into a sense of tragic emptiness and loss, conveyed by both Versailles and the captive swan.

However, while Moore presents a dying Versailles to be mourned, she also plants the seeds for the next stanza: part of what is to be mourned is the swan's captivity. In the second stanza, the harder consonants and the multi-syllabic words convey a renewed vigor as the swan, a Venus or a phoenix, seems to rise up from "the branching foam / of polished sculptured / flowers." Indeed, the first stanza would seem in retrospect to be a softening, romanticizing mirror for the actual present artifact in the second stanza. The "miscellany" of strange things—"tree of cockscomb / tinted buttons, dahlias, [and] seaurchins"—are the "everlastings," and not the culture, which gave rise to them. [24] Moore's very invention of the word "everlastings" conveys the changed vision, from a Versailles which would be seen as a symbol of eternal qualities to an existence in which such lofty qualities are "noun-ized" into particular, literal manifestations.

By not attempting to establish her authority through cultural mirrors, Moore has moved assuredly through changing visions—visions which locate the cause for their own decentered consciousness, "The king is dead." In many ways, Moore attains the kind of seeing that Pound is attempting to effect in "Hugh Selwyn Mauberly." That she succeeds where he fails well be because her speaker is not attempting to achieve a conclusive or even a provisional identity through the objects of her contemplation. The poem's subtle but absolute execution allows for an understanding of the delicate but revolutionary shift caused by the death of all internal and external kings: "that which is great because something else is small."[25]

3 / "ADVERSE IDEAS":

From Bryn Mawr to Early "Observations"

An art is vital only so long as it is interpretive, as it manifests something which the artist perceives at greater intensity and more intimately than his public. . . . The
problem in so far as it concerns Provence, is simply this:
Did this "chivalric love," this exotic, take on mediumistic
properties? Stimulated by the color or quality of the
emotion, did the "color" take on forms interpretive of the
divine order?

—Ezra Pound, *The Spirit of Romance* (1910)[1]

I have been reading the tragic Comedians wild dissipa-
tion—and the wildest wine I have ever tasted sure—Its
[sic] the flower of passion fine and no mistake—Love stories are as stories of course drivel—It is the glint of the
actual that appears now and then that grabs hold of you.

—Marianne Moore, Letter to family (1908)[2]

Of her early writing, Moore commented that she
began writing in response to "adverse ideas."[3] The term "adverse
ideas" is particularly appropriate for Moore's early poetry, for it captures the frequently oppositional stances of her pre-1918 poetry as
well as the opposing ideas and languages that make up individual
poems. As early as her undergraduate years at Bryn Mawr (1905–
1909), Moore begins to develop an aesthetic that is anti-symbolic
and anti-specular. However, it is not until 1915 that Moore's poetry
manifests its characteristic complexity and verbal prodigiousness and
that she begins publishing in such major literary periodicals as the
Egoist, *Others*, and *Poetry*.

Perhaps one of the greatest contradictions between the critical reaction to Moore's work and the actual reality of her poetic endeavor is the impression that she wrote with little or no regard for the larger literary tradition.[4] The extent of Moore's literary as well as non-literary reading, as evidenced by her reading lists at Bryn Mawr, her personal notebooks, and critical prose is very impressive. However, despite her extensive reading, Moore at this time of her life experienced herself as disconnected, commenting in an interview with Donald Hall: "I was rather sorry to be a pariah, or at least that I had no connection with anything."[5] Indeed, the extremity and the inventiveness of Moore's early poems manifest the extent of her alienation, and her literary ambition.

The difficulties of Moore's poetic venture—of a Modernist attempting to construct a universal consciousness out of a "direct treatment of the 'thing,'" and of a woman attempting to write a universal poetry that includes her perspective—cannot be stressed enough. Moore's incapacity to take on the authoritative conventions of an earlier masculine literary tradition and her refusal to assume a position of secondariness in writing a poetry of "plaint," of the "blues," or of "abandonment," left her with a severe lack of resources.[6] Up until 1915 Moore's poetry consisted of verse forms that make their statements rather tersely; this limitation was not the product of an uneducated or resourceless mind, but of a very real lack of resources.

I suggest that Moore's early poetry developed from its pre-1915 brevity to a rich, verbal complexity through her discovery of two modes which enabled her to produce a poetry of ambiguity and multivalency—the modes of contrariety and of the fantastic. The term "contrariety" denotes for Moore the desirable condition in which two opposing terms or both sides of a contention are equally true. The word "contrarieties" first appears at the bottom of her manuscript, "Masks," also titled "A Fool, A Foul Thing, A Distressful Lunatic." This "adverse" poem corrects the one-sided derogatory meanings which have accrued to the goose, the vulture, and the loon. At the bottom of her manuscript page, Moore has typed, "The place where contrarieties are not equally true is nothing to me."[7] While Moore's poem itself does not enact an aesthetic of contrariety, but of opposition to stereotypic conceptions of the goose, vulture, and loon, perhaps a dissatisfaction with the didactic, one-sidedness of her own correction suggested the desirability of a double truth. An admirer of Blake, to whom she wrote several, almost all unpublished, poems during this period, Moore may well have derived her notion of contrarieties from Blake's "contraries." But whereas for Blake contraries dynamically articulate and empower one another, for Moore contrarieties result far more frequently in paradoxes and conundrums—in self-canceling or "duplicitous" speech, disclosing unresolvable contradictions. [8]

Moore's mode of the fantastic, sometimes found in the same poems as her mode of contrariety, further extends her play of meanings, creating uncertainty as to whether the events of her poems are to be taken as natural or supernatural and whether their languages are to be read on a literal, allegorical, or symbolic level.

Discussions by Tzevtan Todorov and Christine Brooke-Rose concerning the fantastic in literary texts are highly useful in considering Moore's poetry of this period. Tzvetan Todorov in *The Fantastic* has defined the fantastic as a nineteenth-century genre in which the reader experiences the events described as neither natural nor supernatural, but "hesitates" between possibilities. As soon as one possibility is elected over the others, the fantastic ceases to exist. For Todorov, the fantastic is an expression primarily of a suppressed and unarticulated psychology: "The fantastic must have something of the involuntary about it, something submitted to—an integration as troubled as it is troublesome, rising suddenly from a darkness which its author was obliged to take just as it came." The fantastic exists only in the nineteenth century, for in the twentieth century its troubling darkness is replaced by psychoanalysis. [9] Christine Brooke-Rose in her *A Rhetoric of the Unreal* has argued for the existence of the fantastic or unreal in the twentieth century. Maintaining that Todorov's definition of the fantastic actually heralds much of twentieth-century literature, Brooke-Rose emphasizes the uncertainty arising from a larger crisis in which "reality" is increasingly difficult to locate and define. For Brooke-Rose, the reader's hesitation does not occur only with respect to whether an event is natural or supernatural, but whether to read texts on a literal, allegorical, or symbolical level. [10]

For Moore, both the modes of contrariety and of the fantastic open up a play of meanings which enable her to encounter and engage in symbolic discourse while maintaining a position "elsewhere." That is, Moore can engage the meanings of the larger literary tradition and system of representation without having to assume a singular or identificatory (specular) stance. Moore's modes of contrariety and of the fantastic are highly inventive attempts to construct textual realities that bespeak her and to address corresponding troubling psychological dilemmas—her anxiety at becoming an author. Indeed, much of Moore's "adverse" poetry concerns itself, on the one hand, with the uses and misuses of language, and, on the other hand, with those persons and power structures which inspire and prohibit her expression. Frequently, then, Moore's poetry of contrariety provides a critique of the system of representation and a way of situating herself within it. Her poetry of the fantastic manifests more directly her psychological discomfiture at assuming a position of authority within a literary tradition that discourages, when it does not prohibit, women's accession to powerful speaker and writer roles.

Notably, throughout this early "adverse" writing, Moore is consciously worried about the need for continuity and embodiment. While as a woman poet visited by "adverse ideas," Moore is critical of literary conventions and forms of representation, her criticism is threatening to her for she has so little "body"—tradition and conventions—from which to write. The ultimate threat of any critique is, of course, that it will disqualify, disembody, that upon which its critique ultimately depends. While through the modes of contrariety and of the fantastic Moore works to establish an embodied poetry from an "elsewhere," several of her poems from this period directly concern themselves with issues of embodiment and continuity.[11] In one early unpublished poem with the conflicted and remarkable title "He did Mend it. His body / Filled a Substantial In- / terstice," Blake is praised for "spanning" a "fissure in the earth."[12] In "Diligence Is to Magic as Progress Is to Flight," Moore creates a protagonist whose language itself is embodied, inseparable from things: "Speed is not in her mind inseparable from carpets. Locomotion arose / in the shape of an elephant; she clambered up and chose / to travel laboriously."[13] And as already discussed, "Those Various Scalpels," written near the end of the period under discussion, contrarily and fantastically critiques a dissection "more highly specialized than the tissues of destiny itself," while utilizing a poetic convention which dissects a whole body.

In establishing the methods of contrariety and of the fantastic as a means of poetic composition, Moore can embody "adverse ideas." That is, rather than assuming a singular critical stance with respect to that which she dislikes or refuses, Moore can enter into the play of meanings which articulate and define her existence, whether she likes them or not. In a sense, Moore, inharmoniously situated within the larger literary tradition, is seeking a means of writing a poetry of harmonious equilibrium. However, in order to do so as a woman, she establishes forms of ambiguity which disclose and confound, rather than blend and unify, differences.

As early as her years at Bryn Mawr, Moore's writing, and her thinking about writing, are distinguished by their "adversity." Throughout her letters home, an insistent commentary runs about her fear and joy "in wielding the pen," which she frequently expresses as contrition and rebelliousness about the forms her writing should take.[14] Even though she worries about the failure of her writing to achieve "coherence," to make a "point," or to promote certain values, she also flaunts these supposed weaknesses.[15] And while she complains of her short stories that she cannot "hit on anything unashamedly rousing and real," she endorses her story "Pym" as "nothing but a series of individual impressions," and will commend another one of her stories as what "Dr. D. would call a 'tentative story.'"[16] In response to her mother's critical comparison of Moore's work with another Bryn Mawr student's work, Moore grants that her writing does not uphold certain religious values, but defends the validity of her own "distracting influences": "Ruth writes better and thinks better than I but that she 'feels' better I am not willing to confess. . . . She is mature in method and attitude and so on but not 'susceptible' as far as I know to distracting influences, devils, wildness, and so on."[17]

Although Moore elects to call her own incompatibility with received thoughts and values her "susceptibility . . . to devils, wildness, and so on," her early writing in fact represents a highly thoughtful encounter with the literary tradition and representational system. Indeed, many of her earliest poems address the issue of how to locate and establish something real or actual, a project that takes her in two different directions. On the one hand, she will explore the virtues of a plain and explicit diction and a concomitant sense that things are as they appear; and, on the other hand, she will engage in highly ambiguous language and "byplay" with a corresponding sense of reality as illusive.[18] A poem such as "Things Are What They Seem" establishes the reality of what seems to be the unalterable case by stating it in no uncertain terms:

The cloud between
Perforce must mean
   Dissension

The broken crock's
Condition mocks
   Prevention[19]

However, in "My Senses Do Not Deceive Me," while seeming to uphold the validity of sensuous experience, Moore raises the distinct
possibility that language may have its own powerful reality apart
from its referent:

Like the light of a candle
   Blown suddenly out,
I witness illusion,
   And subsequent doubt.
Like a drop in the bucket
   And liquid as flame,
Is the proof of enjoyment
   Compared with the name.[20]

Although on one level the poem would seem to be lamenting that
enjoyment itself is largely illusory, it also suggests that the word "enjoyment" has far more staying power than anything to which it might
refer.

Moore's first published poem at Bryn Mawr, "To Come After a
Sonnet," includes both of Moore's impulses—to speak plainly and to
engage in illusive "byplay." Composed as a response to "A Sonnet," a
portrait of Moore written by her classmate, Mary Nearing, "To Come
After a Sonnet" is clearly a reaction to Nearing's archaic and romantic
address to Moore, which includes such lines as:

Thou shouldst have lived in that far vanished time
That lingers in old fading tapestry. . . .
. . . thou, a high-born dame in ancient hall,
Hadst sat among thy maidens, silent all
Or low voiced, clothed in garments
Of palest green, thy braids of red-gold hair,
Touched by the high-built casement's guilded beams
While soft-stringed music brought thee waking dreams.[21]

In contrast, Moore's poem (published in the same issue of Bryn Mawr's literary magazine as "A Sonnet") employs plain diction, light rhyme, and "inconsequential" "meanings":

> A very awkward sketch, 'tis true;
> But since it is a sketch of you,
> And then because I made it, too,
> I like it here and there; —do you. [22]

Moore's poem would seem impelled to playfully undo the gilded composure of her friend's poem through the addition of her own tripping verse. In making the initial assertion that Nearing's portrait better depicts its maker than its subject, she then suggests that perhaps both poems together provide a "sketch," if not a portrait, of both persons. Moore would seem to be suggesting that the "here and there," or the thesis and antithesis, of their poems as a single collaborative poem better captures both makers—their "elsewhere"—than could any single, fixed portrait.

While Moore does not directly address her difficulties in writing poetry as a woman within a masculine literary tradition, she does record a sense of recognition that she is up against a great deal. In her poem "Perseus to Polydectes"—also titled at different times "Progress," "Conservatism," and "I May, I Might, I Must"—the speaker's problem is decidedly not her will to accomplish the described feat, but her inability to decipher the difficulties of her task:

> If you will tell me why the fen
> appears impassable, I then
> will tell you why I think that I
> can get across it, if I try. [23]

The changing titles of the poem, especially from "Progress" to "Conservativism," suggest Moore's unclear sense of what to make of the endeavor at hand. Furthermore, the title "Perseus to Polydectes" indicates that for Moore the "impassable fen" is at least in part an allusion to the difficulty of writing poetry: Perseus, rescued from a sea chest by Polydectes, was sent to conquer Medusa; when he cut off Medusa's head and the blood soaked into the earth, Pegasus, the winged steed of poetry, was brought forth.

At this time, Moore directly conveys her fear or dread of writing in two poems: "To a Screen Maker" and "To My Cup-bearer." Although her fears are not evident in the published version of "To a Screen Maker," an early version associates "making" with "Horrid doubt," "grim doubt," and "Hot folds afloat . . . / forms of doubt."[24] Moore's "To My Cup-bearer" anticipates many of her poems of the fantastic in its veering between a natural and supernatural event, and between a familiar and oracular voice:

> A lady or a tiger-lily,
> Can you tell me which,
> I see her when I wake at night,
> Incanting like a witch.
> Her eye is dark, her vestment rich
> Embroidered with a silver stitch,
> A lady or a tiger-lily,
> Slave, come tell me which?[25]

The poem is noteworthy for even at this very early stage (1908) of Moore's writing, it shows how her problems with a central speaker and her inability or refusal to stay within the perspective of the "I" begins to open into the mode of the fantastic. Unable to determine the nature of the frightening apparition for herself, the speaker asks the help of a "you," and/or a "slave." While such figures as a "lady or a tiger-lily" abound in men's writings as either idealized muses or frightening apparitions, Moore's same-sex status makes identification difficult. In this poem, she evades the issue by interjecting another presence and asking this "slave" to answer her question. However, the poem's forced final line, extremely uncharacteristic of Moore even at this early stage, reveals the poem's ultimate irresolution.

Although Moore's earliest poetry manifests a commitment to ambiguity and byplay, it is not until such poems as "Reticence and Volubility," "Critics and Connoisseurs," "My Apish Cousins," and "Injudicious Gardening" that she makes "contrariety" or a doubleness of meaning a primary structure in her poems. Indeed, as already noted, the singular didacticism of her adverse stance in "A Fool, A Foul Thing, and A Distressful Lunatic" may well have prompted her to conceive of the possibility of contrarieties. However, between the singular stance of "A Fool, A Foul Thing, A Distressful Lunatic," and the contrariety of such poems as "Critics and Connoisseurs" and "My

Apish Cousins," Moore composed "Diogenes," a poem in which "contrariety" is mentioned but is not a principle of composition. The poem is revealing, for it would seem to be inspired by something of Blake's conception of contraries, while falling short of Moore's eventual concept of and practice of contrariety. In "Diogenes," as in "A Fool, A Foul Thing, A Distressful Lunatic," Moore wishes to overturn conventional wisdom concerning the moral superiority of religious asceticism and the moral depravity of sensuous richness. Through the use of one of asceticism's primary tools, logic, Moore corrects the notion that sensuous richness is connected to moral depravity:

> Day's calumnies,
> Midnight's translucencies.
>   Pride's open book
> Of closed humilities—
>   With its inflated look;
> Shall contrarieties
> As feasible as these
>   Confound my wit?
>
> Is Persian cloth
> One thread with Persian sloth?
>   Is gold dust bran?
> Though spotted Ashtaroth
>   Is not a Puritan,
> Must every gorgeous moth
> Be calico, and Thoth
>   Be thanked for it?[26]

Although Moore inverts the hierarchical dualism between asceticism and sensuousness, as does Blake, she also largely reinscribes them. Moore herself may well sense an unspecified lack in her poem, rhetorically asking, "Shall contrarieties / As feasible as these / Confound my wit?" In the last analysis, the poem is a didactic, if skillful, rebuttal of a didactic belief.

In "Reticence and Volubility," Moore achieves a poem which not only enlists the idea of contrariety, but implements it. In establishing an opposition between a reticent Merlin, who practices magic, and a voluble Dante, who follows tradition, Moore reveals the limitations of both ways, creating a conundrum of impossible choices:

"When I am dead."
The wizard said,
   "I'll look upon the narrow way
   And this Dante.
     And know that he was right
     And he'll delight
       In my remorse,
       Of course."
"When I am dead,"
The student said,
   "I shall have grown so tolerant,
   I'll find I can't
     Laugh at your sorry plight
     Or take delight
       In your chagrin,
       Merlin."

Neither the wizard nor the student is superior or inferior. While the wizard upon his death will regret his extravagant approach to knowledge at the expense of the "narrow way," the student who has followed the "narrow way," traditional knowledge, will suffer an excessive tolerance and so will be unable to take delight in Merlin's chagrin. The possibilities that the wizard and student represent are not dynamic complements, but cancel each other.

Indeed, for Moore who, despite her avid reading, had not yet found her way, the contest between the reticent Merlin and a voluble Dante is a significant one. That she achieves a perfect standoff between them acknowledges her desire and need for both the representable and the unrepresentable. In fact, throughout her life Moore continues to feel a tension between reticence and volubility, writing in 1924 of her poetry's "recalcitrance and undesirable expansiveness," and in 1949, as already quoted, "when I am as complete as I like to be I seem unable to get an effect plain enough."[27] Initially Moore titled this poem "The Wizard in Words," signalling her own sense of achievement in this poem, but also tipping the balance of the poem towards Merlin. As "Reticence and Volubility," the poem's assertions, defined with respect to each other, are held in equilibrium, enabling Moore to position herself, neither "here" nor "there," but "elsewhere."

In "Critics and Connoisseurs," Moore extends the dialectical opposition that "Reticence and Volubility" sets in play. But now the contest is between a critic of "conscious fastidiousness," represented by the swan who acts according to preconceived principles, and of the connoisseur ant of "unconscious fastidiousness," who acts according to impulse. While criticism of this poem has frequently addressed the issue of which side wins, establishing various rationales for both outcomes, it has tended to concentrate on consciousness versus unconsciousness, rather than the complex phenomena designated by Moore—"conscious fastidiousness" and "unconscious fastidiousness."[28] In both instances, "fastidiousness" itself denotes a certain kind of reasonable and unreasonable behavior, complicating the terms "conscious" and "unconscious." And, it is finally the complex behavior, not the simple designation, which interests Moore. "Critics and Connoisseurs" offers a critical, sympathetic, and ultimately comic portrayal of both its swan and ant, showing them as stalemated in their respective behaviors.

In depicting the swan, Moore moves from a formal to an informal diction, mocking the pretensions of the swan as well as demonstrating conscious and unconscious uses of language, characteristic respectively of the deliberate thinking of a critic and the spontaneous judgment of the connoisseur:

> I remember a swan under the willows in Oxford
>   with flamingo colored, maple-
>   leaflike feet. It reconnoitered like a battle
>   ship. Disbelief and conscious fastidiousness were the staple
>   ingredients in its
>   disinclination to move. Finally its hardihood was
>   not proof against its
>   proclivity to more fully appraise such bits
>   of food as the stream
>
> bore counter to it; it made away with what I gave it
>   to eat.

While the swan's behavior is determined by a critical reluctance to ingest that which is foreign to it, finally its curiosity and/or hunger gain prominence and "it made way with what I gave it / to eat." After the formal build-up and the description of the swan who "reconnoitered like a battle / ship," the simplicity of the action and corresponding change in diction provide a marked contrast. This transformation demonstrates the necessity and desirability of unreasoned and spontaneous behaviors, a "coming to know," that is the root meaning of the word "connoisseur," thereby revealing the "connoisseur" in the swan and making way for the ant. Indeed, Moore reveals how the swan's conscious fastidiousness is accompanied by a necessary unconsciousness that is, at least in this instance, more nurturant than its "disinclination to move."

However, in turning next to describe the ant as a representative connoisseur, its more spontaneous behavior, rooted in the virtues of its own experience, is also criticized:

> Happening to stand
> by an ant hill, I have
> seen a fastidious ant carrying a stick, north,
> south, east, west, till it turned on
> itself, struck out from the flower bed into the lawn,
> and returned to the point
>
> from which it had started. Then abandoning the stick as
> useless and overtaxing its
> jaws with a particle of white wash pill-like but
> heavy, it again went through the same course of procedure.

While appropriately the unpretentious ant is presented through a more straight-forward speech than Moore uses for the swan, its simple action, unproductively repetitive, is mocked. However, despite the potential ridiculousness of both the swan's and the ant's behaviors, it is their determination, their "fastidiousness," that Moore values, praising in the beginning of her poem other such behaviors: "a / mere childish attempt to make an imperfectly / ballasted animal stand up" and "a similar determination to make a pup / eat his meat on the plate."

The poem concludes with an unanswerable question, offering a critical but fond last look at the arbitrary, aggressive, and humorous activities of swan and ant:

> What is
> there in being able
> to say that one has dominated the stream in an

attitude of self defense,
in proving that one has had the experience
of carrying a stick?

It has been suggested that the critic addressed as "you" in the poem
may be Moore's mother, who actively criticized Moore's work.[29] If so,
the ant could well be a stand-in for Marianne herself, who, although
frequently collaborating with her mother on her poems, could also
be disheartened by her mother's criticism.[30]

In "My Apish Cousins," later titled "The Monkeys," Moore creates
a standoff between the speech or language of a connoisseur-type figure or artist and a critic or critical public.[31] One of the subtexts for
this investigation is the implied contradiction between a magnificence that is remembered dimly. The speaker proclaims, "I recall their
magnificence, now not more magnificent / than it is dim. It is difficult
to recall the ornament, / speech and precise manner of what one
might call the minor acquaintances twenty / years back." However, in
contrast to this initial assertion, the speaker remembers at least one
acquaintance, Gilgamesh, with extreme particularity—his "wedge
shaped, slate-gray marks" as well as his protest speech. The unclear
referents of this speech (presumably a critical "they" and an artistic
"it") coupled with its sublime diction add to the poem's conundrum,
creating a dimness that is magnificent and a magnificence that is dim:

> "They have imposed on us with their pale
> half-fledged protestations, trembling about
> in inarticulate frenzy, saying
> it is not for us to understand art; finding it
> all so difficult, examining the thing
>
> as if it were inconceivably arcanic, as symmet-
> rically frigid as if it had been carved out of chrysoprase
> or marble—strict with tension, malignant
> in its power over us and deeper
> than the sea when it proffers flattery in exchange for
> hemp,
> rye, flax, horses, platinum, timber, and fur."

While, on the one hand, Gilgamesh would seem to elect to disman-
tle the critical vocabulary that would create distance between a

perceiver of art and a work of art, on the other hand, he wishes to enlist it to maintain art's powerful defamiliarity—to maintain its dim magnificence. In fact, this particular dilemma is stated quite clearly as a contradiction in Moore's later poem "Picking and Choosing": "Literature is a phase of life; if / one is afraid of it, the situation is irremediable; if / one approaches it familiarly / what one says of it is worthless." While Gilgamesh's speech begins in protest against the representation of art as "inconceivably arcanic," he uses an arcane vocabulary to create an image of art that is "deeper than the sea," capable in its "flattery"—its idealizing mirror—of winning a contest against such basic riches as "hemp / rye, flax, horses, platinum, timber, and fur." While "it" (art) thereby seems very substantial—as idealizing mirror its exchange value is greater than "horses" or "platinum"—it also seems very insubstantial—mere "flattery." Indeed, these contradictory possibilities are disclosed in Moore's "contrarious" writing as the potential sublimity and vacuity of symbolic art—its magnificence and dimness.

While "My Apish Cousins" explores contradictory concepts about art, "Blake" and "Injudicious Gardening" (originally titled "To Browning") are structured around contradictory perspectives and in this way anticipate Moore's later poetry of collage. In "Blake," the two perspectives—of Blake looking at "us," and of "us" looking at Blake—are mediated through the tentative assertions of an "I," delimiting further the powerful presence of the sun-like Blake:

> I wonder if you feel as you look at us,
> As if you were seeing yourself in a mirror at the end
>   Of a long corridor—walking frail-ly.
> I am sure that we feel as we look at you
> As if we were ambiguous and all but improbable
>   Reflections of the sun—shining pale-ly. [32]

Although in "Blake" Moore represents the "us" as more ambiguous and improbable than Blake, the poem's deliberate tenuousness subtends the discussion of this giant from the past in a not-altogether-disappearing-way. "Frail-ly" and "pale-ly" assert their own idiosyncratic delicacy into a world where some presences crudely outshine others—a shadow world where the concept of "contraries" may be insufficient to demark the complex reality of the "contrarieties" of a woman poet.

In "Injudicious Gardening," Moore's double perspective leads to a far more duplicitous and complicated verbal action. The poem begins by upholding the literal yellow rose over its derogatory symbolic association with infidelity, much as she does for the loon, goose, and vulture in "A Fool, A Foul Thing, and A Distressful Lunatic." But in "Injudicious Gardening," this adverse idea is only part of Moore's agenda. For while the poem addresses the betrayal of the literal yellow rose by its symbolic associations, it also considers another possible betrayal, of Elizabeth Browning by Robert Browning, or perhaps more generally of women by men:

> If yellow betokens infidelity,
>   I am an infidel.
>   I could not bear a yellow rose ill will
>   Because books said that yellow boded ill,
>   White promised well;
>
> However, your particular possession—
>   The sense of privacy
>   In what you did—deflects from your estate
>   Offending eyes, and will not tolerate
>   Effrontery.

In Moore's notes, she cites the instigating incident for her poem as Robert Browning's effort to remove the reproach of the yellow rose by planting white:

> Letters of Robert Browning and Elizabeth Barrett; Harper. Vol 1, p. 513; "the yellow rose? 'Infidelity,' says the dictionary of flowers." Vol. II, p. 38: "I planted a full dozen more rose trees, all white—to take away the yellow-rose reproach!"

"Injudicious Gardening" is a curious poem. Initially criticizing Browning for succumbing to traditional and public symbolism, the second stanza turns to praise him for his "sense of privacy." And while praising his "sense of privacy," Moore exposes him. Moore's discovery of the instigating incident represents a case of true biblio-detective work. In order to uncover the full event, Moore had to put together two entries from two different volumes of Browning's letters. On one manuscript copy of the poem, Moore wrote in a note to herself, "It is not positively stated that the yellow bushes were 'dug up.'"[33]

Why, one might ask, if Moore respects Browning's privacy and even questions the facts on which her poem is based, does she dig up this incident and make it an occasion for public perusal? Her title "Injudicious Gardening" would seem to refer to several failures in judgment—Robert Browning's possible sexual betrayal of Elizabeth; his compliance with the symbolic register at the expense of the literal; and Moore's own nosey gardening, her writing of this poem. It is hard to tell how critical Moore is of Browning—upholding her own private feelings about yellow roses over his conformity with the symbolic register, flaunting her own effrontery in a poem while praising his sense of privacy. That Moore should both praise privacy and disregard it reveals a deep need to cross the boundaries between the private realm—which often constrains women—and the public—which often excludes her. Inviting the reader into the original garden, Moore restages the first sin: the woman has seen, but not seen, the naked betrayal of the man as he hastily covers his guilt with his symbols.

In addition to the poems of contrariety, the period of 1915–17 is distinguished by the production of poems of the fantastic. Indeed, the mode of the fantastic extends the play of meanings set in motion by the poems of contrariety—causing uncertainty as to whether the events in the poems are to be understood as natural or supernatural, and whether the language is to be read as literal, allegorical, or symbolical. Certainly, such poems as "Those Various Scalpels" and "My Apish Cousins"—structured around contradictory perspectives and concepts—also partake of the fantastic in their more than natural but not quite supernatural events and in their mélange of languages. However, the great majority of Moore's poems in the mode of the fantastic can be grouped together on the basis that they are written as forms of address to a "you"—usually an artist or entity whose manner of expression is at issue—who Moore either admires or condemns.

Several critics have remarked on the numerous poems of address written during this period; however, they have not explored these works with regard to Moore's attempts to locate herself with reference to an existing literary tradition or her anxieties surrounding her belief in a writer's necessary egoism.[34] Notably, only a few of Moore's poems of address to a "you" she admires—her poems of praise— employ the mode of the fantastic, while all of her poems addressed to a "you" she condemns—her poems of blame—are written in the mode of the fantastic. Laurence Stapleton characterizes the poems of this period as "witty declarations addressed to a person or creature who is always addressed as 'you' and whose possible reply or reaction has no seeming relevance to [Moore's] own observations."[35] Although Stapleton does not differentiate between Moore's poems of praise and her poems of blame, her characterization is particularly appropriate for the poems of blame, which so emphatically deliver their dread at the thought of their others that they themselves seem silenced in the end.

Sandra Gilbert and Susan Gubar in *The Madwoman in the Attic* have characterized women's acts of authorship as beginning in dis-ease and dread, for in becoming an author at all a woman must deny and destroy constructs of feminine identity.[36] In addressing powerful masculine figures, Moore's poems of praise and blame allow her to confront her own desires and fears for power. By distinguishing good power from bad power—power as "gusto" and power as force— Moore can begin to define for herself a kind of power which is acceptable and necessary. But perhaps, more importantly, Moore's poems of the fantastic allow her to express a censored or repressed psychology—one which remains suppressed in the dominant psychology of our own day—of a woman's need to look at a man in the knowledge of the disconnection that he and his language mean for her and to overpower that disconnection. Moore, who felt herself to be a pariah at this time in her life, created in defense a host of masculine pariahs—beatifically and horrifically decked out in strange motlies of quotations and languages.

Most of Moore's poems of praise, including "To a Man Working His Way Through a Crowd," "To a Strategist," "To William Butler Yeats on Tagore," and "To a Prize Bird", deliver their eulogies in relatively plain, dignified language. Only two—"George Moore" and "To the Peacock of France"—employ the mode of the fantastic. Moore's straightforward, somewhat earlier, poems of praise are far less personal confrontations with powerful figures than affiliative eulogies designed to articulate and affirm Moore's own evolving ideas about the character of the artist and the purpose of art. Moore commends her addressees for their powers of resistance as well as of integration. "To William Butler Yeats on Tagore" praises Yeats for his staunchness, "by virtue of which he says // the thing he thinks—that it pays / to cut gems even in these conscience-less days."[37] In "To a Prize Bird," Moore commends George Bernard Shaw for not being "blinded by the chaff / That every wind sends spinning from the rick." And even as a "colossal bird," he is integrated into a larger life, for "No barnyard makes [him] look absurd." Moore praises Disraeli in "To a Strategist" for his capacity not only to maintain himself against others, but to integrate with them due to his "chameleon-like," "particolored mind." In Moore's poem to Gordon Craig, "To a Man Working His Way Through a Crowd," she confronts the relationship between unreason and power in artistic endeavors. She commends Craig: "The most propulsive thing you say, / Is that one need not know the way / To be arriving." She also notes that "undoubtedly" Craig "overbears," but concludes: "one must do that to come where / There is a space, a fit gymnasium for action."[38]

In "George Moore" and "To the Peacock of France," Moore's desire to affiliate herself, not only with the principles embodied in the writings of George Moore and Molière but with the writers themselves, is enacted through the fantastical events and dictions of these poems. Both poems manifest a kind of erotic competition in which Moore seems to be saying, "I know you at your most subtle and profound and I will demonstrate my respect and love for your writing by literalizing you, revealing you as indelibly you." In the poems, Moore seems intrigued by the men's association with illicit worlds and activities, but also apologizes for them. In "George Moore," Moore addresses her namesake with intense knowingness; she has not been put off by, but has seen deeply into, his "transparent-murky, would-be-truthful 'hobohemia' ":

> In speaking of 'aspiration,'
> From the recesses of a pen more dolorous than blackness,
> Were you presenting us with one more form of
> imperturbable French drollery,
> Or was it self directed banter?

Habitual ennui
Took from you, your invisible hot helmet of anemia
While you were filling your little glass from the
decanter
Of a transparent-murky, would-be-truthful
"hobohemia"—
And then facetiously
Went off with it? Your soul's supplanter,
The spirit of good narrative, flatters you, convinced that
in reporting briefly
One choice incident, you have known beauty other
than that of stys, on
Which to fix your admiration.

The speaker asserts that she is not deceived by George Moore's predilection for "stys," for despite his subject matter, the compression of
his narrative in "one choice incident" reveals his knowledge of
beauty. Moore obliquely reasons that George Moore's "habitual ennui" disarmed him, for unable consistently to maintain ennui in a
state of ennui, he is supplanted by his own "spirit of good narrative."
The speaker of Moore's poem addresses George Moore as one writer
to another. And if her speech seems to take place in this world, it also
seems to be happening in another world, a kind of land of the dead
where men and women meet in much candor, and equality.

Moore establishes this equality through her poem's exaggerated
wit and its compounded and murky associations. Not wanting to
merely dispel George Moore's dark made of light, but to "unspell"
it—to "come / At the cause of the shouts"—she plays with his language and meanings.[39] In the notes, Moore quotes from George
Moore's writings the likely instigating occasion for her poem: "We
certainly pigged it together, pigs no doubt, but aspiring pigs." Moore
in her poem carries through on the contradictions in being "aspiring
pigs," playing with the word "pen." Certainly, a "pen" is a home for
pigs, prisoners, or other debased sorts who are kept or who keep
themselves from the free commerce of life. As such, this pen may be
related to the concentrated isolation of writers. As a writing tool, the
pen is surely an instrument of aspiration, resembling, as a thing filled
with ink, the hollow needle and syringe used in medical aspiration

to remove fluid, such as pus or serum, from a cavity of the body.
Moore is removing the "pus" from George Moore's " 'hobohemia,' "
"going off with it," "unspelling" the "stys" that affix his beauty.

In "To the Peacock of France," written to Molière, Moore would
seem to wish to outcharm Molière by rapid-fire statements that move
without discrimination between abstract statements and literal embodiments. As with "George Moore," the speech event itself seems
neither of this world nor of another world, but in the poem's terms
exists as a playful "rant[ing] / up and down through the conventions
of excess." One of Moore's influences in creating the mode of the
fantastic may be the exaggerated speech found in the dialogues of
such Russian novelists as Turgenev and Gogol, and copiously transcribed in her notebooks. [40] As in "George Moore," "To the Peacock
of France" employs such contradictory terminology as "black-
opalescent" and "jewelry of sense" in order to establish its own irreducible knowingness of Molière:

> In "taking charge of your possessions when you saw them," you
> become a golden jay.
> Scaramouche said you charmed his charm away,
> But not his colour? Yes, his colour when you liked.
> Of chiselled setting and black-opalescent dye,
> You were the jewelry of sense;
> Of sense, not license; you but trod the pace
> Of liberty in market-place
> And court.

As Moore praises Molière, she uses images that subliminally suggest
the sculptured splendor of a peacock: "golden jay," "charm," "chi-
selled," "black-opalescent dye" (the peacock's eye-like spots), "jewelry," and "trod the pace . . . in market-place." Consequently, by the
end of the poem, the convincing unfurling of the peacock's tail is as
much a credit to Moore's sleight of hand as it is to Molière's writing.
While Molière has charmed the rogue Scaramouche's color away,
Moore herself has charmed Molière's hidden color into being:

> You hated sham: you ranted up
> And down through the conventions of excess:
> Nor did the King love you the less
> Nor did the world,

In whose chief interest and for whose spontaneous
delight, your broad tail was unfurled.

Unlike Moore's poems of praise, all of her poems of blame form
around fantastical events and through fantastical languages. As in
"George Moore" and "To the Peacock of France," Moore would seem
to wish to inscribe each entity as literally and indelibly itself through
and through. But rather than using her wit and talent for the purpose
of affiliation, in the poems of blame she employs them to disaffiliate
herself, absolutely. Through her speaker's dread and loathing of these
figures, Moore not only defines for herself what she dislikes, but actually tells off a number of powerful entities—identifying their
power as crude, arbitrary, and destructive. Certainly in part, Moore
is defending herself against the masculine powers of a larger literary
establishment, or more generally, from the masculine bias of the
larger representational orders. Against these masculine Medusas,
Moore delivers her own powerful Medusa speech. As one pariah to
another, Moore voices her dread as familiar and as oracle.

In these poems, power which asserts itself in the absence of a life-
originating and -respecting motivation or which is devoid of an at-
tentive and large response is castigated. Moore's first published poem
of blame, "To the Soul of 'Progress,'" appeared with her poem of
praise, "To a Man Working His Way Through a Crowd" in *The Egoist*
as her first publication in a major literary magazine. But whereas in
"To a Man Working His Way through a Crowd" Moore apologizes
for Gordon Craig's "overbearance," in "To the Soul of 'Progress,'" also
titled "To Military Progress," all apology for power is eradicated by
the dread and loathing she expresses at the very thought of "Military
Progress." Moore faults her addressee, for its mind acts apart from its
body—a spectre of disembodiment. As a literal, allegorical, and
symbolic presence on this landscape, this "Soul" is all mind:

> You use your mind
> Like a mill stone to grind
>   Chaff.
> You polish it
> And with your warped wit
>   Laugh

At your torso.
Prostrate where the crow—
  Falls
On such faint hearts
As its God imparts—
  Calls

And claps its wings
Till the tumult brings
  More
Black minute-men
To revive again,
  War

At little cost
They cry for the lost
  Head
And seek their prize
Till the evening sky's
  Red.

Through this fallen Ozymandias, Moore suggests that the mind's very capacity to abstract itself from the body—whether the body of the past, the body politic, or an actual body—leads to war and destruction. Indeed, as does Adrienne Rich much later, Moore suggests that war itself may be caused by certain "masculine" forms of thinking.

Moore's familiar and oracular voice in this poem, as in other poems of blame, is a version of what Alicia Ostriker has referred to as the "ekoskeletal" style of many contemporary women writers. But whereas Ostriker explains the hard, rigidifying qualities of this voice through R. D. Laing's idea that the "ontologically uneasy" person may take on the characteristics of the oppressor as a kind of will to power, an alternative or complementary explanation is that a woman writer's voice may lack resonance because it lacks meaningful cultural contexts in which to amplify itself, subtly and significantly.[41] And in Moore's poems of blame, she makes a decided strength of this lack.

As in "To the Soul of 'Progress' " the entities portrayed in "The Pedantic Literalist" and "To Statecraft Embalmed" are cut off from a life-originating and -respecting motivation. And in these poems, their absence of "good" motivation leads respectively to a literal and figurative woodenness and frozenness; the Pedantic Literalist and Statecraft Embalmed follow rigidly and frigidly certain rules of conduct. In the "Pedantic Literalist," motive and conduct are misaligned, for the Pedantic Literalist says "unkind / Things with kindness, and the most / Irritating things in the midst of love and / Tears." "Presenting an obstruction / To the motive that it served," the "core" has itself turned to wood:

> What stood
> Erect in you has withered. A
> Little "palm tree of turned wood"
> Informs your once spontaneous core in its
> Immutable production.

The poem begins with a reference to "Prince Rupert's Drop," an item which appears in Brewer's *Dictionary of Phrase and Fable*, owned by Moore: "Their form is that of a tadpole. The thick end may be hammered pretty smartly without its breaking, but if the smallest portion of the thin end is nipped off, the whole flies into fine dust with explosive violence."[42] Although the Pedantic Literalist's dull underside protects him from destruction, if tampered with in the wrong way, he will explode. Moore mimics the Pedantic Literalist's rigid dullness, inscribing him as indelibly himself by concluding her second and fourth stanzas with the unresounding repetition of the phrase "immutable production."

In "To Statecraft Embalmed," Moore attacks a kind of statesmanship of "discreet behavior" which is "not now the sum / Of statesmanlike good sense." While the immediate provocation for this poem may well be the kind of statesmanship which precipitated World War I (it was published in 1915), it broadens its reflection to include anything which is an "incarnation of dead grace." As the Pedantic Literalist suffers from an all but wooden pulse—a "carved cordiality ran / To and fro . . . like an inlaid and royal / Immutable production"—Statecraft Embalmed as a dead symbol of justice possesses a frozen pulse:

> O
> Bird, whose tents were "awnings of Egyptian
> Yarn," shall Justice' faint, zigzag inscription—

Leaning like a dancer—
   Show
The pulse of its once vivid sovereignty?
You say not, and transmigrating from the
   Sarcophagus, you wind
    Snow
Silence round us. . . .

In the Ibis' frozen removal from life, he cannot fully recognize himself and thereby unwittingly commits suicide, an act which occurs in the unseen recesses of his throne:

   Slow
To remark the steep, too strict proportion
Of your throne, you'll see the wrenched distortion
   Of suicidal dreams
    Go
Staggering toward itself and with its bill,
Attack its own identity, until
   Foe seems friend and friend seems
    Foe.

By presenting Statecraft Embalmed and the Pedantic Literalist as literal embodiments of their own principles, Moore can inscribe their destruction as self-inflicted, for as she writes of the Pedantic Literalist, they "invite destruction."

In "To a Steam Roller" and "To Be Liked By You Would Be a Calamity," Moore takes to task two more entities which are arbitrary and unfeeling in their exercise of power. The poems are likely inspired by a literary or art establishment that does or might misunderstand Moore's work, as the poems include quotations which link them respectively to an actual critic and a fictional critic. "To a Steam Roller" was most likely inspired by the critic Lawrence Gilman's comments, cited in Moore's notes and copied down at greater length in her notebooks: "We have endeavored . . . to be clinical, strictly impersonal— momentarily ignoring the fact that an impersonal judgment in aesthetic matters is a metaphysical impossibility."[43] But as frequently occurs in her poetry, Moore uses Gilman's words against him as well as those who would induce conformity under the aegis of impersonality:

The illustration
is nothing to you without the application.
    You lack half wit. You crush all the particles down
        into close conformity, and then walk back and forth on
            them.

Sparkling chips of rock
are crushed down to the level of the parent block.
    Were not "impersonal judgment in aesthetic
        matters, a metaphysical impossibility," you

might fairly achieve
it. As for butterflies, I can hardly conceive
    of one's attending upon you, but to question
        the congruence of the complement is vain, if it exists.

Insulting the steam roller as a "half wit" who imagines himself capable of transcendent points of view, the speaker suggests that the
steam roller can't even get the illustration without the application
and so proceeds to apply her illustrative metaphor of steam roller:
"You crush all the particles down / into close conformity, and then
walk back and forth on them." However, although the speaker in
applying her illustration comes down to the steam roller's own level,
so to speak, she establishes an important distinction. While Moore
criticizes the steam roller for a lack of imagination that keeps him
within the realm of the literal without realizing it, Moore herself
enacts her imaginative respect for the literal, the particularity and
thingness of things. That is, by creating a metaphoric steam roller
that steam rolls, Moore refuses to hierarchize symbolical and literal
meanings, breaking with the conventional use of the literal as mere
illustration for the symbolical.

In contrast to her steam-rolled application of the steam roller,
Moore through a leap of judgment, inserts a butterfly, which she
holds out as a possible complement to the steam roller. Whereas the
steam roller would presumably only attend to an impersonal certainty, the personal "I" is happy with a tentatively stated complement.
However, it is "vain" to question the "congruence of the complement,"
for in the world of the steam roller any tentativeness is sure to meet
destruction. Indeed, Moore's poem may well be a criticism of contraries which neutrally co-exist, of comfortable paradoxes, for in an

existence in which the arbitrary powers of steam rollers can be determining, opposites do not mutually define a single reality but as contrarieties reveal very real contradictions. Notably, when "To a Steam Roller" was first published in *The Egoist*, as well as in its subsequent publication in *Observations*, it immediately preceded "Diligence Is to Magic as Progress Is to Flight," which affirms an aesthetic practice that must dwell particularly with things—"locomotion is not inseparable from carpets"—rather than above them.

In "To Be Liked By You Would Be a Calamity," originally titled "To the Stand Patter," the speaker encounters another steam roller type, but one even more fantastically sketched—as "feet" "that . . . would like to feel" her "flesh" beneath them. The absence of any distinguishing features of the poem's combatants other than their feet and flesh, and the explosive staccato delivery create an impression of "irreducible strangeness":

> "Attack is more piquant than concord," but when
>   You tell me frankly that you would like to feel
>   My flesh beneath your feet,
>   I'm all abroad; I can but put my weapon up, and
>   Bow you out.
> Gesticulation—it is half the language,
>   Let unsheathed gesticulation be the steel
>   Your courtesy must meet,
>   Since in your hearing words are mute, which to my
>   senses
>   Are a shout.

As in "To a Steam Roller," Moore uses a quotation against its source, writing a poem in which "attack" is decidedly un-"piquant." The speaker's response to this "stand patter" is to resort to bodily lines of defense—"gesticulation"—and to increase her circulation—"I am all abroad." As do Irigaray, Cixous and others, Moore establishes her bodily responses as her last line of defense and increases her "circulation" through a mixture of languages—archaic and contemporary, abstract and concrete. Robert Pinsky has remarked that this poem is "an elaborate way of saying "'I am not speaking to you'—or more accurately, 'I am not speaking to that person.'"[44] It may even more accurately be saying "I am not speaking within your (or that) frame of reference." Unlike her previous poems of blame, "To Be Liked By You Would Be a Calamity" creates its defense primarily through its speaker's powerful self-assertion, rather than through her portrait of an entirely despicable "you." But like the other poems, its staged event seems both natural and supernatural, and its mélange of languages create uncertainty as to whether the poem is to be read literally, allegorically, or symbolically.

The quotation with which the poem begins is taken from Hardy's novel *A Pair of Blue Eyes*. Even though Moore admired Hardy, she does not seem to have appreciated his narrational commentary at the end of a chapter in which the protagonist, Elfride Swancourt, is more compelled by the negative review of her first novel than a reassuring letter from her distant fiancé. Chapter XV concludes with Elfride's meditations on a stranger who like the "you" in "To Be Liked By You Would Be a Calamity," is "without name or shape, age nor appearance":

> Attack is more piquant than concord. Stephen's letter was concerning nothing but oneness with her: the review was the very reverse. And a stranger with neither name nor shape, age nor appearance, but a mighty voice, is naturally rather an interesting novelty to a lady he chooses to address. When Elfride fell asleep that night she was loving the writer of the letter, but thinking of the writer of that article.

Although Elfride writes her novel, *The Court of Kellyon Castle*, a medieval romance, under the pseudonym of Ernest Field, her sex has been more than suspected by the reviewer, Henry Knight, who finds the historical romance not at all up to his standards: "We found ourselves in the hands of some young lady hardly arrived at years of discretion, to judge by the silly device it has been thought worth while to adopt on the title-page, with the idea of disguising her sex." While Knight praises the novel for its "murmuring of delicate emotional trifles," he faults it for failing to "weld" "to stirring incident a spirited variety of elemental human passions." Later, meeting Elfride, Knight will advise her to confine herself to writing about domestic scenes.[45] As the novel proceeds, Elfride breaks off her engagement with her fiancé, becomes engaged to Knight—an engagement called off because of untoward circumstances—and eventually meets an untimely death by falling off a wall.

The attack on Elfride's novel, Elfride's love for her attacker, their unhappy separation, and the lugubriousness of the novel's ending must have played on Moore's imagination. The high-spirited protagonist may well have reminded Moore of herself, who while at Bryn Mawr wrote fiction set in a medieval time. Knight's criticism of the novel is similar to criticism made by Moore's teachers at Bryn Mawr, her mother, and Moore herself concerning her inability, in her fiction, to "hit on anything unashamedly rousing and real."[46] Furthermore, as a child Moore had been teasingly called by her classmates, "Marianna of the Moated Grange," and at the age of four she had leaned against a shutter and fell out of a second story window.[47]

Elfride and *A Pair of Blue Eyes* were in fact the impetus for at least one of two earlier poems by Moore. By looking at these poems in conjunction with "To Be Liked By You Would Be a Calamity," different dimensions of Moore's anxiety of authorship, as it emerges throughout her poems of blame, can be observed. Although no reference is made to *A Pair of Blue Eyes* in the first of these poems, "My Lantern" (1910), it contains similar images and the same rhythm as the second poem, "Elfride, Making Epigrams," probably written about 1914.

Both "My Lantern" and "Elfride, Making Epigrams" reveal Moore's uncertainty and anxiety about writing. In "My Lantern," the voice, as it does in the later fantastic poems, veers between that of a familiar and that of an oracle. Notably, it is not the speaker who performs artistic feats, but "my lantern" or "my light":

> The banners unfurled by the warden
> Float
> Up high in the air and sink down; the
> Moat
> Is black as a plume on a casque; my
> Light,
> Like a patch of high light on a flask, makes
> Night
> A gibbering goblin that bars the way—
> So noisy, familiar, and safe by day.[48]

The poem is full of ambiguity. The "banners unfurled," for instance, create a sense of freedom as well as captivity, in so far as it is the warden who unfurls them. Furthermore, it is unclear whether the lantern reveals night as less fearful than one might expect—only "a gibbering goblin . . . familiar and safe by day"—or as a perpetual and gruesome night which only appears safe by day. In "My Lantern" Moore may well be enacting her own ambivalence at the site of her creativity—an ambivalence which confounds light and dark, free-dom and captivity, safety and danger. Indeed, part of Moore's fasci-nation here, as in several of her later poems, is to explore and repre-sent the phenomena of a shade of difference, of black on black, and white on white: the / Moat / . . . black as a plume on a casque," and "a patch of high light on a flask."

In "Elfride, Making Epigrams," the warden has disappeared from the poem, but the allusion to imprisonment remains in Elfride's actual encasement in the scene.

> Devices as slender as pennons float
> Up high in the air and sink down; the moat
>   Encases her head like a casque;
>   Her light
>   Sorties, like high lights on a flask,
>   Requite
> Men with torrents of toads from lips of lead
> And then grind up her bones to make their bread.

In writing a note for the poem, Moore foregrounds Elfride's fictional novel, rather than Hardy's novel, as her source:

> "The Court of Kellyon Castle, A Mediaeval Romance by 'Ernest Field', (Elfride Swancourt)—reviewed by Henry Knight in *The Present*. See A Pair of Blue Eyes by Hardy. [49]

The poem is confusing, for while it is titled, "Elfride, Making Epi-grams" and states that "Her light Sorties . . . / Requite / Men with torrents of toads from lips of lead," it is the men or possibly the "light Sorties" which grind up *her* bones to make *their* bread. Elfride, encased in the scene, would seem to be both subject and object, perpetrator and victim, of her writing.

In contrast to these earlier poems, in "To Be Liked By You Would Be a Calamity," the speaker directs her attack entirely outward. Now the "lips of lead" have become "unsheathed gesticulation." The speaker has entirely removed her body as the material basis for men's discourse, by making it her own means of bodily and unreasoning self-expression. She need not stand pat at being evaluated by such "Stand Patters" as Knight or even Hardy, but can defend herself through her own "gesticulation" and "circulating" languages. For she realizes that she is not being heard—not because of any deficiency in her character or expression—but because in their hearing "words are mute, which to / [her] senses / Are a shout."

As Moore turned from writing poems of blame addressed largely to a male or masculine "you," she produced three poems addressed to at least partially feminine presences—"Those Various Scalpels," "Roses Only," and "Sojourn in the Whale." Of these, "Those Various Scalpels" (as discussed in Chapter 2) provides the most complicated conundrum of "adversity." In the poem, Moore, engaging modes of both contrariety and the fantastic, and employing a poetic convention that cuts up the body while asserting the importance of a whole "destiny," praises and blames a male or female entity, who is subject or object, and fearful or fearsome. "Those Various Scalpels," written at the very end of this period, well reveals the problems encountered and inventions employed as Moore attempts to situate herself in a predominantly masculine and specular literary tradition—in which the languages/scalpels that allow her articulation are also the weapons which can destroy her.

In contrast to the poems addressed to a masculine "you," "Roses Only" and "Sojourn in the Whale" address a feminine "you" more simply and intimately, and less fantastically. In "Roses Only," Moore makes comical the very possibility of a natural beauty existing merely as an object for men's contemplation by addressing the rose as if it possesses understanding. Appealing to the rose through the logic of "what-must-be-the-case," the speaker deliberately ignores the traditional rose's pristine aura of beauty beyond understanding, and instead affirms the rose's intelligence over its beauty, its subjectivity over its objectivity. In an intimate tone the speaker chides the rose for pretending to be a "delightful happen-so" who could survive with "nothing of preeminence:"

> You do not seem to realise that beauty is a liability rather than
> an asset—that in view of the fact that spirit creates form
>   we are justified in supposing
>   that you must have brains. For you, a symbol of the

           unit, stiff and sharp,
conscious of surpassing by dint of native superiority and
           liking for everything
self-dependent, anything an

ambitious civilisation might produce; for you, unaided to
           attempt through sheer
     reserve, to confute presumptions resulting from observation
           is idle. You
           cannot make us
     think you a delightful happen-so. But rose, if you are
           brilliant, it
     is not because your petals are the without-which-nothing of
           pre-eminence. You would, minus thorns,
look like a what-is-this, a mere

peculiarity. They are not proof against a worm, the elements,
           or mildew
     but what about the predatory hand? What is brilliance
           without co-ordination? Guarding the
     infinitesimal pieces of your mind, compelling audience to
     the remark that it is better to be forgotten than to be
           remembered too violently,
your thorns are the best part of you.

   What is affirmed about the rose are her thorns—her active qualities of assertion, intellect, and self-protection. While these "pre-
eminences" are symbolized by the thorns themselves, they are also
present in the essential thorniness of the flower as a "symbol of the
unit, stiff and sharp" and as "self-dependent" as well as in its "dint"
and its "infinitesimal pieces." Moore's thorny languages of litigation
and the marketplace further undo the rarified atmosphere in which
the rose traditionally dwells, as do the falling rhythms of her opening
periodic sentences which land flatly on "must have brains" and "is
idle." However, by titling her poem "Roses Only," Moore suggests
that her poem is not for or about those cynics who would attempt to
undo the sweetness and beauty of the rose, but rather for and about
roses who would find themselves sweeter for their "co-ordination"—
their beauty *and* thorniness. For it is not the rose's thorns which are
her peculiarity, but she herself without them.

If "Roses Only" addresses the problem of women's representation as other by establishing the subjectivity, assertiveness, and intelligence of such a traditionally feminine other as the rose, "Sojourn in the Whale" addresses the problem of "every kind of shortage" with which feminine presences, such as Ireland, must contend. "Sojourn in the Whale" is one of Moore's few published poems of feminine complaint. However, it is a complaint that enacts its own victory over those "men" who would patronize Ireland's struggles, failing to take any responsibility for her "shortages," but rather blaming them on her "feminine temperament" and "native incompetence." And while the poem is ostensibly about Ireland, it is also probably about Moore, who was Irish, and her artistic struggles:

> You have been compelled by hags to spin
> gold thread from straw and have heard men say: "There is
> a feminine
> temperament in direct contrast to
>
> ours which makes her do these things. Circumscribed by a
> heritage of blindness and native
> incompetence, she will become wise and will be forced to
> give
> in.

In addition to having "to spin gold from straw," several other enterpries that Ireland's temperament purportedly makes her do are "Trying to open locked doors with a sword, / threading the points of needles, planting shade trees / upside down." Each of these magical, fairy-tale endeavors involves an activity in which the physical properties of the "things" present an "obstruction to the motive that they serve," but are also enhanced by their unusual use. That is, while the poem conveys the frustration inherent in these endeavors, it also relishes their magical improbability. While the length and threat of a sword make it hardly the tool to open a locked door, it is intriguing to imagine the turning of such a small mechanism as a lock with the even smaller, distant tip of a sword. Likewise, while it is impossible to thread the eyeless point of a needle, the familiar difficulty of threading needles is intensified by imagining a thread pointing at the narrow, unperforated end. And shade trees indeed become trees of the shade if they survive a planting which would place their dense foliage pointed down into an even denser earth.

John Slatin in *The Savage's Romance* discusses "Sojourn in the Whale" as an example of Moore's struggle to maintain "an imperviousness" that in the end is overwhelmed by "common experience" and acknowledgment of her indebtedness to the larger literary tradition. At this time in her life, argues Slatin, Moore is dependent on her isolation as a form of self-protective identity and so willfully guards it. Like Ireland, Moore is obtusely still "trying to open locked doors with a sword."[50] However, in not taking into account the alienating languages in which Moore as a woman must write—her representational as well as other material "shortages"—Slatin fails to appreciate both the dimensions of Moore's struggles and the extent of her achievement in this poem. Moore's felt isolation is her shared "feminine experience," and thus her relation to the literary tradition is necessarily oblique. As is Ireland's art, Moore's art lies in diligently carrying through impossible feats—attending to without falsely resolving the contradictions that structure her literary endeavors, and her existence. Indeed, Moore's imaginative care in conceiving impossible feats caused by "shortages" reveals her desire to share the "common experience" of feminine and oppressed others.

The poem concludes with a wonderful image of rising water. Like the complacent "men's" speech set "in motion" in such poems as "To a Steam Roller" and "To Be Liked By You Would Be a Calamity," the men's patronizing observation about water set "in motion" is their own undoing:

> ". . . she will become wise and will be forced to give
> in. Compelled by experience, she
>
> will turn back; water seeks its own level": and you
>   have smiled. "Water in motion is far
>   from level." You have seen it when obstacles happened to
>   bar
> the path—rise automatically.

The water is the poem's own rising anger, coolly stated. However, it is not an anger bent on convincing those who would find the anger only another example of a "feminine / temperament," but an anger intent on washing away what it did not originate, rising as freely and as spontaneously as a smile. It is a "byplay more terrible in its effectiveness / than the fiercest frontal attack."[51] It is Moore's "white ink"; her laugh of the Medusa.[52] And while this poem is motivated by considerable anger, it rises above this anger in its imaginative portrayal of feminine activity that is finally superior to the usual functioning of swords, needles, and shade trees—warring men, domesticated women, and established knowledge.

4 / "AGREEING DIFFERENCE":

Middle "Observations"

It is not always possible to tell whether a man or a woman is designated in certain of the poems and this is as it should be; in so far as a poem is a work of art, one does not wish to know, and must not know too definitely, the facts which underlie its expression.

—Marianne Moore, *The Dial* (1921)[1]

There seems to be almost too great a wish to be transparent. . . . .

—William Carlos Williams, *The Dial* (1925)[2]

In 1917–18 Moore's aesthetic begins to change from one of "adverse ideas" to one of "agreeing difference."[3] The poetry of address gives way to a poetry of description, and the combative voices and fantastical diction of the earlier poetry are replaced by a seemingly agreeable manner and more ordinary language. While in such poems as "An Egyptian Pulled Glass Bottle in the Shape of a Fish" and "The Fish," Moore's writing would seem to wish to attain the same kind of unmediated seeing that also compelled her Modernist male peers, the problem of perspective—and its inevitable mediation—surfaces at the same time. For Moore, of course, as a woman, an unmediated seeing is particularly problematic in its presumption that the "direct treatment of the 'thing'" will yield a commensurate consciousness. And while all of Moore's male peers will find an unmediated seeing problematic, none so quickly and radically encounters this problem in precisely Moore's terms—as an inability to see clearly and to express the "genuine."

Several of Moore's poems composed at this time directly address the problem of perspective. "In the Days of Prismatic Colour" attributes the loss of clarity and a singular perspective to the addition of Eve to Adam's life. When "Adam was alone," there was "nothing to modify" color "but the mist that went up." Then, but no longer, "obliqueness was a variation of the perpendicular, plain to see / and account for."[4] "A Grave" begins with the double problem of seeing the sea when a man is blocking the view and when there is no secure footing or vantage point from which to consider it:

> Man looking into the sea,
> taking the view from those who have as much right to it
>   as you have to it yourself,
> it is human nature to stand in the middle of a thing
> but you cannot stand in the middle of this

Moore's perhaps best known poem, "Poetry," can itself be seen as a poem caught between mediated and unmediated seeing—seeing that begins in "adversity" and also wishes to express the genuine. Beginning with "I, too, dislike it," Moore suggests that poetry may be redeemable in that there is in it, after all, "a place for the genuine," but she is discontented with any writing of the genuine, as her multiple revisions of the poem attest.[5]

Moore partially resolves the difficulty between a mediated and an unmediated seeing—between an adverse and agreeing perspective— in her poetry of lists and collage, methods employed in many of her most significant poems, including "When I Buy Pictures," "People's Surroundings," "Silence," "Marriage," "An Octopus," "Sea Unicorns and Land Unicorns," and "No Swan So Fine." Unlike earlier poems in which Moore establishes her difference through singular speakers promulgating a barrage of languages, in these poems Moore establishes her difference, her "elsewhere," by playing language against language more variously—utilizing a range of voices and intensities. She can simultaneously affirm phrases that have been "said in the very best way" and relativize them through ironic juxtapositions that deliberately misuse or misread them.[6] That is, Moore can attain the very expansiveness and agreeableness of one situated within a "universal" poetics while investigating and expressing her own alienation from its centrist vision.

I locate Moore's aesthetic as changing noticeably in 1917 because of her new emphasis on not "entangling" herself "in the negative."[7] Although in her earliest writing Moore utilizes negative positions, as her writing and poetry evolve forms of negativity are largely eclipsed. While this preference for expressing negative judgments through indirection and omission may be due at least in part to particular religious, familial, and educational influences, importantly, Moore's "predilection" for positive statements necessitates that she rework literary and language conventions—if she is to express herself *as* a woman.

Moore's changing regard for Edgar Allen Poe throughout 1911–1917 provides a clear indication of her evolving aesthetic. In an unpublished poem addressed to Poe, written sometime before 1915, Moore praises his capacity to create new "warped" worlds.[8] However, in her 1916 unpublished essay, "Poe, Byron and Bacon," Moore begins rejecting Poe, criticizing him for entangling himself in the negative; he and Byron do not "uphold the affirmative rather than the negative aspects of a contention." But while she criticizes Poe's negativity, she praises his (and Byron's) writing style without reservation: "In their moods of flaming gorgeousness and white hot paroxysms of contempt the manner is often perfect while the matter disappoints."[9] Later, in her essay "The Accented Syllable," Moore further restricts her admiration of Poe. Although she praises his writings for their "distinctive, written, personal tone of voice," she criticizes his style for its "tincture of artificiality. . . . There is a slight grandiloquence, a straining for rarity, and an unmistakable tone of condescension."[10] Notably, Moore writes her last fantastic poem of simple contempt in 1916.

In Moore's prose written after 1916, a new aesthetic emerges— one that holds that neither the sensibility of the artist nor the object of contemplation should outweigh the other. Moore's statements promote a kind of Eliot-like "objective correlative" crossed with Stevens' (at that time unpublished) concept of "evasion."[11] In an unpublished review of William McFee's *Casuals of the Sea* (1916–17), she writes, "when we say that we have much to be thankful for in the attitude of mind which an author has brought to bear on his work, we, in the main, concur with him, and when we say that the subject matter of the book is not so interesting as the author's attitude of mind, we are simply saying that the author has not reached perfection."[12] For exactly the opposite reasons, Moore criticizes John Dos

Passos' *Three Soldiers*: in this case the problem is not that the sensibility exists apart from its object of contemplation, overwhelming it, but that it is too distanced and noncommittal. Dos Passos "has the sensitiveness of the photographic plate without the harmonizing faculty of disciplined judgment. . . . We do not feel the loss of John Andrews in his supposedly tragic end, as great either to himself or the world. . . . A great deal of intellectual power is required to make defeat a satisfactory theme."[13]

In Moore's poetry of this time, we find her meditations seemingly limited to their objects of contemplation. By making a single " 'thing' " ("whether subjective or objective") the focus of her poems, Moore can establish a nominal coherence and therefore authority. In her "adverse" poetry Moore frequently relies on forms of address as a means of establishing her authority and "rant[s] up and down through the conventions of excess." But in her poetry of "agreeing difference" she establishes her authority through "proper" attention to an object or subject. Whereas in her earlier poetry the sensibility of her speakers is prominent, she now rejects a point of view which is either in excess of or in deficiency of its object. And, by giving the object as much importance as the subjective response to it, Moore frees herself from those demands for discursive coherence that confine her poetry to existing thought and argument. She thereby, in Williams' words, is able to increase the "multiplication of impulses that by their several flights, crossing at all eccentric angles, might enlighten."[14]

In order to show how Moore's poetry of "agreeing difference" evolved, I consider in the next two chapters several different kinds of poems which more or less chronologically replaced each other. In this chapter, I first discuss those poems in which the problem of perspective is thematically addressed. I then turn to poems that portray objects and scenes in largely visual, and seemingly unmediated, ways. Moore wrote several poems, including "The Fish" and "An Egyptian Pulled Glass Bottle in the Shape of a Fish," which appear to be relatively simple "seeings." In these poems Moore seems to avoid her difficult problems with perspective by restricting her poetic vision to what the eye can actually see. However, the poems move from visions which emphasize transparent qualities to visions which emphasize opaque qualities. In their preference for opacity and in other preferences as well, the poems involve themselves in the symbolic implications of their seeing and in what I argue is a feminine and feminist reworking and subverting of values. I conclude this chapter by considering Moore's poems written in the form of lists, as the key to her collage poems. In these and the collage poems, discussed in the next chapter, Moore, in order to create her "agreeing" poems, engages a multiplicity of perspectives, creating a fluid écriture—"a sea of shifting" with "no weather side."[15]

Most of Moore's poems published between 1918 and 1921 are either meditations on perspective and artistic vision or are direct seeings. Images, on the one hand, of light, transparency, and clarity, and on the other hand, of darkness, opacity, and deflection are prominent. Beginning frequently in desire for the former and the related values of "simplicity, harmony, and truth," these poems usually conclude by establishing the opposite and the values of particularity, complexity, and tentativeness. Although in her prose writings of this time Moore frequently upholds qualities of transcendence and universality, when these values are put to the test in her poetry, they are undermined. And while at this time Moore is turning away from syllabic verse toward free verse, seemingly in an effort to clarify and simplify her writing, her meanings do not reflect this same transparency.[16] Indeed, Moore is struggling to attain the Modernist edict of "direct treatment of the 'thing,'" but her own position in the culture as a woman leads her to write an indirect, complex poetry.

In "Poetry" and "In the Days of Prismatic Colour," the conflict between mediated and unmediated seeing is addressed thematically. Both poems postulate the prior existence of an original clarity or truth. "In the Days of Prismatic Colour" locates this time historically as co-existing with Adam: "Not in the days of Adam and Eve but when Adam / was alone." In "Poetry," this clarity and truth is expressed as "the genuine," which exists prior to and apart from its representation in poetry. Although both poems manifest a belief in, or perhaps merely a nostalgia for, an original and originating truth and clarity, neither purports to inscribe these qualities. In fact, both poems enlist opposing terms—"sophistication" and "complexity" in "In the Days of Prismatic Colour" and "the fiddle" of poetry in

"Poetry"—and are caught up in the very qualities they initially seem to denounce.

While critics have puzzled over "Poetry," defining its central terms in quite divergent ways, "In the Days of Prismatic Colour" has typically been discussed as a poem that illustrates Moore's predilection for simplicity and truth over complexity and sophistication.[17] But like "Poetry," "In the Days of Prismatic Colour" exists far more significantly in its tensions than in its resolutions. In "In the Days of Prismatic Colour," truth undergoes a sea change in its passage through the birth canal ("throat") of sophistication of Moore's poem.

The poem begins with a sense of an enticing clarity that exists

> Not in the days of Adam and Eve but when Adam
>   was alone; when there was no smoke and color was
> fine, not with the fineness of
>   early civilization art but by virtue
> of its originality; with nothing to modify it but the
>
> mist that went up, obliqueness was a varia-
>   tion of the perpendicular, plain to see and
> to account for: it is no
>   longer that; nor did the blue red yellow band
> of incandescence that was color keep its stripe

The addition of Eve brings "smoke" and "complexity," upon which the poem comments:

>   complexity is not a crime but carry
> it to the point of murki-
>   ness and nothing is plain. complexity [sic]
> moreover, that has been committed to darkness, instead of
>   granting it-
>
> self to be the pestilence that it is, moves all a-
>   bout as if to bewilder us with the dismal
> fallacy that insistence
>   is the measure of achievement and that all
> truth must be dark.

Typically, these lines have been glossed as Moore's statement that complexity itself is dark; whereas the lines state that complexity

"that has been committed to darkness"—a stifled or obscured complexity—produces the "dismal fallacy" that "all / truth must be dark."
This statement precisely leaves open the possibility that complexity
given over to itself, allowed to be "the pestilence that it is," may not
be "dark," may even possess some stripe, if not exactly the "blue red
yellow band" of the world before Eve. Moore implicitly suggests that
Eve's inclusion has made an unbreachable difference to the world in
which "obliqueness" can no longer be "a variation of the perpendicular." And since a singular clarity is no longer possible, Moore urges
that the complexity of a fallen world—a world no longer possessed
of the prelapsarian light of Adam alone—must be seen for what it is.

While this poem, in its concern with unmediated and mediated
seeing, is part of Moore's "agreeing" poetry, it also bears resemblance
to the fantastic poems of her earlier work. Like those earlier poems,
the depiction seems neither quite natural nor supernatural, and it
moves between literal and symbolic registers, maintaining their dis-
tinctness and thereby creating uncertainty. Sophistication, allied
with complexity, turns into a palpitating monster, which, metamor-
phosing into a wave, leaves the residue of a quite literal truth:

> Principally throat, sophistication is as it
>   al-
> ways has been—at the antipodes from the init-
>   ial great truths. "Part of it was crawling, part of it
> was about to crawl, the rest
>   was torpid in its lair." In the short legged, fit-
> ful advance, the gurgling and all the minutiae—we have the
>   classic
>
> multitude of feet. To what purpose! Truth is no Apollo
> Belvedere, no formal thing. The wave may go over it if it likes.
> Know that it will be there when it says:
>   "I shall be there when the wave has gone by."

Although Moore describes sophistication as being at the opposite
ends of the "initial great truths," importantly it is as "throat," merely
another part of the same body of which the great truths form the feet
(podes). The depiction of "sophistication" "as principally throat"

becomes clearer by referring to the source from which the quotation "part of it was crawling . . ." is taken:

> Part of it was crawling, part of it was about to crawl, and the rest was still torpid in its lair. But it thirsted and put its jaws in the stream. Then all Cephisus ran into them, and horrid gurgling sounded in its throat. As the water sunk, often did the nymphs lament for Cephisus that was no more. [18]

Like the monster in the fragment, Moore's sophistication is "Principally throat" presumably because it consumes rather than replenishes. However, her "throat"/ "sophistication" also seems capable of replenishment for it is associated with the concluding wave through its own wave-like motion and water-like "gurgling." Indeed, in this poem it seems that sophistication is the wave that passes over "truth," leaving it brightly intact. The concluding truth, however, is not the kind of pervasive clarity posited at the beginning of the poem. Now truth exists as a kind of deposit or residue, almost one of the gurglings and minutiae of sophistication. (In an earlier version of the poem, both truth and sophistication are depicted as possessing multiple feet.)[19] However, it is a truth completely identified with itself and separate from a larger context, just as quotation marks separate its utterance from the main body of the poem. [20]

While critics such as Stapleton have called attention to the majesty and "calm assurance" of the ending—truth partaking negatively of the Apollo Belvedere it rejects—the ending also leaves an impression of bathos, as if truth is speaking about itself, rather than being delivered. [21] The rejected Apollo Belvedere appears by contrast to be a falsifying attempt to approximate the singular light which Moore establishes at the beginning of her poem as existing no more. Moore rather elects an estranged, inexpressible, truth—an "it" which has emerged through the sophisticated workings (throat) of her poem.

In "Poetry," Moore turns decisively away from the modes of contrariety and the fantastic, though the poem shares other characteristics of Moore's earlier adverse poetry. Moving between address and description, she begins with her best known (adverse) line, "I, too, dislike it," and attempts, but fails, to provide a definition of poetry that is not "entangled in the negative." The terms and examples Moore uses to define poetry proliferate in a relation of supplementarity rather than unity, as can be seen in the displacement of "genuine" from the primary term to be investigated at the beginning of the poem to one of two terms—along with "raw material"—at the conclusion of the poem. Furthermore, Moore's implied audience changes from those who seem to have every right to dislike poetry to those who earn, through appropriate attention to poetry, the honorific comment: "then you are interested in poetry." The beginning and ending of the poem are as follows:

> I, too, dislike it: there are things that are important beyond all
>   this fiddle.
> Reading it, however, with a perfect contempt for it, one
>   discovers in
> it after all, a place for the genuine.

> In the meantime, if you demand on the one hand,
>   the raw material of poetry in
>   all its rawness and
>   that which is on the other hand
>   genuine, then you are interested in poetry.

In "Poetry" Moore is caught between two conflicting impulses: the need and desire to define poetry universally and generally—to "come / At the cause of the shouts"—and to engage irreducible particulars and expressions.[22] While in her later collage poetry she allows whatever positive definition her poems provide to emerge in and through juxtaposed elements, here she is pulled in two directions at once, much like the bat in this poem, "holding on upside down or in quest of something to / eat." Notably, Moore does not attempt to define poetry from her position as maker but as audience—a position that enables her to establish her stance "elsewhere."

Most critics of this poem have noted that for Moore the genuine is an inexpressible quality—"a magnetism, an ardor, a refusal to be false"—which cannot be directly translated into art or the written word.[23] Consequently, this poem is frequently interpreted as an attempt to realize the unrealizable. Establishing this struggle as indeed central to the poem, John Slatin has criticized "Poetry" as another example from Moore's early work in which she refuses "'to go in,' making instead a virtue of her own isolation."[24] Slatin fails to consider that Moore's need to assert her autonomy may in fact be her need to assert her own difference from a poetic tradition and language which do not represent her. Moore cannot achieve the "genuine" in her poetry, for she remains outside the centered vision of a masculinist "universal" poetics that would allow her the semblance of an unmediated "real." While Moore desperately wants to define this activity of poetry that she has given so much of her life to, each assertion is confounded by subsequent assertions, so that it is in fact quite difficult to tell what Moore is recommending as poetry or the genuine. Indeed, Moore writes her definition of poetry largely by spelling out the ways we do not have poetry, as she progressively abandons the definitions and examples she puts forth.

Not only is it difficult to tell what Moore is or is not recommending, but the perspective from which any one aspect of the poem can be considered frequently shifts. For example, after initially praising poetry as "a place for the genuine," Moore lists bodily reactions that seem to be the stimulus for, or the response to, or emblematic of, the genuine, or perhaps all three.[25] Furthermore, as Slatin notes, these examples provide a provisional definition of the genuine even as they are in turn defined by it.[26]

> Hands that can grasp, eyes
> that can dilate, hair that can rise
> if it must, these things are important not because
>   a
>
> high sounding interpretation can be put upon them but
>   because they are
> useful; when they become so derivative as to become
>   unintelligible
> the same thing may be said for all of us, that we
>   do not admire what
>   we cannot understand:

While grasping hands, dilating eyes, and rising hair are associated with the genuine as actions that occur spontaneously and cannot be controlled, they are also laden with associations of gothic fakery and disingenuousness. Furthermore, in that these actions seem to be ends

92

in themselves, it is hard to determine how they could be useful in any common sense of the word, except perhaps in the origination and apprehension of poetry. (Similarly, Moore, in "Picking and Choosing," comments that literature should put us on the "scent"— "a few 'strong wrinkles,' puckering the / skin between the ears.") In adding that a "high sounding interpretation can be put upon them," Moore elevates these particular reactions as potential subject matter for poetry. Noting how these bodily reactions can be "so derivative as to become unintelligible," Moore all but denies them any special status by which they might be seen to aid or exemplify the genuine. Indeed, it would seem that these reactions are particularly prone to disingenuousness, while that behavior which is so peculiar or removed from its stimulus as to seem false, might be closer to the genuine. After noting that "we / do not admire what / we cannot understand," Moore lists in seeming disapprobation actions that, when linked by the conjunction *nor* to "'business documents and school books,'" are then approved of:

> the bat,
> holding on upside down or in quest of something to
>
> eat, elephants pushing, a wild horse taking a roll, a tireless
>   wolf under
>   a tree, the immovable critic twitching his skin like a horse
>   that feels a flea, the base-
> ball fan, the statistician—
>   nor is it valid
>   to discriminate against "business documents and
>
> school books"; all these phenomena are important.

After this elaboration of the genuine, Moore abruptly changes her focus to a discussion of how poetry doesn't occur in the hands of "half poets":

>   One must make a distinction
>   however: when dragged into prominence by half poets, the
>   result is not poetry,
>   nor till the poets among us can be
>   "literalists of

the imagination"—above
insolence and triviality and can present

for inspection, "imaginary gardens with real toads in them,"
shall we have
it.

By recommending that poets should be " 'literalists of / the imagination,' " Moore challenges two poets. In her notes, she credits Yeats as
the originator of this phrase, which he used to criticize Blake in the
essay "Ideas of Good and Evil": "The limitation of [Blake's] view was
from the very intensity of his vision; he was a too literal realist of
imagination, as others are of nature; and because he believed that the
figures seen by the mind's eye, when exalted by inspiration were 'eternal existences,' symbols of divine essences, he hated every grace of
style that might obscure their lineaments." In using Yeats' phrase of
disapprobation as approbation in "Poetry," Moore implicitly criticizes
Yeats' negative assessment of Blake. [27] But in transmuting this phrase
into her own "imaginary gardens with real toads in them," she moves
away from Blake. That is, while Blake, by Yeats' account, does not
distinguish between the reality of the figures of his imagination and
an external reality, Moore reintroduces this duality into poetry. In
"Poetry," we have, on the one hand, "imaginary gardens"—the "fiddle"
of poetry—and, on the other, real things—"'school books'" and
"toads." For Moore, then, a "literalist of the imagination" may be one
who is capable of bringing real things into her poem, which require
special imaginary care lest they be overtaken by an egotistical sublime or specular poetry: "Hands that can grasp, eyes / that can dilate,
hair that can rise." It is interesting to note, in fact, that Moore's poem
is often remembered as the one about "'business documents and
school books'" and "'imaginary gardens with real toads.'" That is, if
Moore's poem puts "'strong wrinkles' . . . between the ears," it does so
by her estranged particulars and not by her comprehensive definitions—despite her ambitious attempt to define poetry in "Poetry."

At about the same time that Moore wrote "In the Days of Prismatic Colour" and "Poetry," which question the very possibility of an
unmediated vision, she composed "An Egyptian Pulled Glass Bottle
in the Shape of a Fish," "The Fish," and "A Grave," which seem to be
poems of "pure" seeings, portraying objects and scenes in predomi-

94

nantly visual terms. Both "An Egyptian Pulled Glass Bottle in the Shape of a Fish" and "The Fish" move from visions of light and transparency to visions of opacity and deflection. "An Egyptian Pulled Glass Bottle in the Shape of a Fish" begins with thirst, patience, and art aligning themselves within the object of Moore's contemplation:

> Here we have thirst
> And patience from the first,
>> And art, as in a wave held up for us to see
>> In its essential perpendicularity;

In the second stanza, as Moore extends her meditation to the "intensity" of art, she portrays its powers of deflection:

> Not brittle but
> Intense—the spectrum, that
>> Spectacular and nimble animal the fish,
>> Whose scales turn aside the sun's sword with their polish.

In a poem that is clearly about need and desire ("thirst"), Moore refuses to depict movement, or to use active verbs, except in the last line. That is, we "have" "patience" and "thirst" and "art." Further, the only active verb, "turn," reveals the deflecting power of the glass bottle "Whose scales turn aside the sun's sword with their polish." Teresa de Lauretis in *Alice Doesn't* has suggested that almost all narratives are hierarchically structured around a male figure whose "desire" allows for narrative action, and a female figure whose "stability" allows for narrative closure. [28] Here, then Moore seems to be subverting the traditional hierarchy that would value movement over stability, by locating activity in stillness—in the surface polish of a fish that can "turn aside" the sun's sword. By turning the object of contemplation into a source of action, she subverts a specular economy in which the other is significant primarily as a mirror or destination for a masculine protagonist.

"The Fish" similarly moves from light to opacity and values the qualities of containment and stillness over those of openness and movement. Beginning with a crystalline seeing of things, the poem concludes with an unclear reference to an "it":

> The barnacles which encrust the
> side

of the wave, cannot hide
there for the submerged shafts of the

sun,
split like spun
    glass, move themselves with spotlight swift-
        ness
        into the crevices—
    in and out, illuminating

the
turquoise sea
    of bodies.

All
external
    marks of abuse are present on
        this
        defiant edifice—
    all the physical features of

ac-
cident—lack
    of cornice, dynamite grooves, burns
        and
        hatchet strokes, these things stand
    out on it; the chasm side is

dead.
Repeated
    evidence has proved that it can
        live
        on what cannot revive
    its youth. The sea grows old in it.

While this poem evokes certain conventional associations common
to poems about the sea—a sense of an ongoing, powerful life; of a
conflicting suffering and death; and of endurance—it ultimately

repels these associations. The seeing is deliberately without depth, without the powers of a specular seeing into things, for as with the edifice, "the chasm side is dead." Indeed, what should be marks of indentation, "lack / of cornice, dynamite grooves, burns / and hatchet strokes," stand out. Further, this "presencing" of still and solid things gives the lines "the / turquoise sea / of bodies" an almost preternatural effect, calling forth a vision of the bodies that inhabit the sea.

The ambiguous "it" in the last stanza intensifies the sense that powers inhere in things rather than in motions, in objects rather than in their symbolic meanings. "It" could well refer to the edifice, a fish, or something unnameable. Like the "truth" at the end of "In the Days of Prismatic Colour" "it" may well be the provisional representation of Moore's impulse to mean more than she can express. As such, "it" is representative of that which resists symbolic incorporation.

In "A Grave," Moore begins with a meditation on the impossibility of seeing the sea, when a "Man looking into the sea" takes "the view from those who have as much right to it as you have to it yourself." Moore calls attention to two difficulties here: the problem of seeing "through" a man, including a man's viewpoint, and the related problem of establishing herself as a centered speaker when she cannot stand "in the middle of this." Moore's depiction of the sea, correspondingly, emphasizes its opacity over its translucency and its surface activities over its symbolic meanings. While Moore may well have written this poem out of a personal crisis that involved thoughts of suicide, the speaker reminds herself that to seek relief in the sea is not to be mirrored in any improved way or to be freed of herself.[29] The speaker works her way out of her crisis by establishing and confronting the actuality or literality of the sea and of death, and her difference from them.

The form of "A Grave" bears an inverse relation to the poetic genre described by M. H. Abrams as the greater Romantic lyric. In the greater Romantic lyric, a speaker resolves his initial sense of crisis through meditation on a natural scene. Typically, the speaker's initial mood of unhappiness or dejection is transformed through an aspect of change in the scene itself—sudden winds, for example, or a clearing sky. Through his meditation, the speaker "achieves an insight, faces up to a tragic loss, comes to a moral decision, or resolves an emotional problem." For Abrams, then, the typical pattern of this kind of lyric is out-in-out; that is, the speaker's attention is first focused outside of himself, then turns inward, and then returns to the world around him.[30] The speaker, in fact, may be seen to possess a highly specular relation to the outer scene, projecting his problems onto it and eventually finding in it a happier reflection.

Moore's "A Grave" reverses this pattern. This poem begins and ends with a short meditation, positing a lengthy scenic description in the middle of the poem. Further, it is precisely through the speaker's separation from the natural scene, which in dominant Romantic iconography is feminine, that she achieves a positive resolution of her crisis.[31] In Moore's poem, the sea prohibits the self-projection and identification prominent in (male) Romantic poems, for it is "quick to return a rapacious look." The sea's "look" is very different from the viewer's gaze, for her "look" can be destroyed:

> There are others beside you who have worn that look—
> whose expression is no longer a protest; the fish no longer
>   investigate them
> for their bones have not lasted:

Whether Moore is alluding to her own thoughts about suicide, or to those of others, she repudiates suicide as a meaningful action. The sea is not a mirroring surface, but an actual grave. Consequently, it is man's surface activity—his particular and careful acts—and not his self-projections, which ultimately save him. Whereas men "lowering nets" unconsciously "desecrate this grave," "as if there were no such thing as death," the speaker of this poem, conscious of the ultimate meaning of penetrating the depths of the sea, trains her vision to the surface:

> The wrinkles progress among themselves in a phalanx—
>   beautiful under networks of foam,
> and fade breathlessly while the sea rustles in and out of the
>   seaweed;
> the birds swim through the air at top speed, emitting cat-calls
>   as heretofore—
> the tortoise-shell scourges about the feet of the cliffs, in
>   motion beneath them

As do greater Romantic lyrics, Moore's poem becomes more intense near the end. But, unlike these lyrics, this intensity causes the speaker to become more conscious of her meditation on the outer scene, as the sound of birds and bell-buoys make "noises" in what has previously been an almost entirely visual representation. The poem resolves its initial questions about perspective and of seeing the sea with an understanding of the opacity of the ocean and what the ocean is not:

> and the ocean, under the pulsation of lighthouse and noise of
> bell buoys,
> advances as usual, looking as if it were not that ocean in
> which dropped things are bound to sink—
> in which if they turn and twist, it is neither with volition nor
> consciousness.

The tone of the ending is intriguing, sounding both of victory and defeat. But it is precisely because of its irresolute and provisional perspective, a perspective that does not claim too much in the face of death, that the poem can reach closure. Importantly, the poem concludes with "consciousness," not "volition," for it is the speaker's unswerving awareness of the sea as a grave and not her will to power over it that allows her to resolve her crisis. Although Pound suggested that Moore invert the order of consciousness and volition to create a stronger ending, Moore elected to keep the order of her words as written. [32] Unwilling to sentimentalize her own personal powers by urging a notion of will in the face of death, the speaker, and presumably Moore, establishes her strength ultimately through her circumspect consciousness of this grave.

The overall effect of this poem is of a kind of containment, as if everything could be known only through its most pronounced boundedness. As a woman, Moore's speaker is traditionally associated with the natural scene and with death itself; Moore resolves her speaker's crisis by establishing the literalness of the sea and death, as entities entirely apart from and different than herself.

In 1920–22 Moore began composing poems based on the format of the list, including "England," "When I Buy Pictures, "New York," "The Labors of Hercules," and "People's Surroundings." As do the poems immediately preceding these, Moore's list poems establish their authority in part through the nominal coherence provided by their "direct treatment of the 'thing.'" However, the format of the list allows Moore to extend her largely visual descriptions and meditations to far more diverse reflections on society and art. Whereas her earlier focus on a " 'thing,' whether objective or subjective," freed Moore from having to make certain kinds of discursive sense, the list form enables her both to maintain this openness, and to reintroduce the ambiguity and multivalency of her earlier poems.

While clearly Moore's list poems approach the fluid writing of a feminine écriture as described by Irigaray and Cixous, among others, they possess a related commitment to a kind of quotidian or "middling" consciousness. Training her reader's consciousness away from the reifications and over-determinations of existing thought, Moore affirms the palpability of phenomena. That is, while Moore wants to keep the edges of phenomena and their defining attributes visible, she also contradictorily desires her reader to see what these edges enclose—the middles or insides. Certainly, Moore's focus on the usual as well as the unusual, rather than on the powerful, is a choice of those objects and qualities which are relatively free from over-determined and reified valuations that overwhelm more fluid realities and possibilities. Indeed, her desire to disclose the very texture of phenomenal and verbal realities makes Moore an important precursor to John Ashbery.[33]

Moore must have been excited by her new format, for she wrote one list poem after the other. The poems themselves include statements about and celebrations of this fluid aesthetic. In "England," Moore honors the "mystery of construction" which "diverts one from what was originally one's / object—substance at the core," and concludes her poem with the "superiority" that may be found in America, flaunting her title "England." In "New York," "commerce" and "accessibility to experience" are validated over "plunder." As Moore works her way through this poem, the pronominal referent for New York becomes amorphous. Initially referring to New York as a location, "it" begins to refer to specific qualities of the city, as if these abstractions were as concretely present as the city itself:

> It is a far cry from the "queen full of jewels"
> and the beau with the muff,
> from the gilt coach shaped like a perfume bottle,
> to the conjunction of the Monogahela and the Allegheney,
> and the scholastic philosophy of the wilderness

to combat which one must stand outside and laugh
since to go in is to be lost.

The shifting or vague referent, like those in many of Ashbery's
poems, suggests that we live not only in places but in words and
concepts.

"The Labors of Hercules" includes the comment that the piano is
"a free field for etching" and that "charming tadpole notes" / belong
to the past." Moore concludes her poem with a list of rather "bald
morals":

                                    one keeps on knowing
"that the Negro is not brutal
that the Jew is not greedy
that the Oriental is not immoral
and that the German is not a Hun."

Whereas in many texts these important moralistic admonishments
are banal precisely because of the ease with which they can be stated
but not observed, in Moore's "free field" the inclusion of this list with
earlier lists defamiliarizes it. In Moore's very complex and shifting
world, the sure pairings of Negro with brutality, Jew with greed, etc.,
seem arbitrary and peculiar associations—stupid "tadpole notes."

In "When I Buy Pictures," the implications of Moore's aesthetic are
reflected in her suggestions concerning how pictures are to be appre-
hended. The poem begins with a self-correction:

When I Buy Pictures

Or what is closer to the truth,
when I look at that of which I may regard myself as the
            imaginary possessor.

Importantly, there is no stated truth, only a correction that is "closer
to the truth." Further, there is no singular stance by which to establish
possession; at most, one is "the imaginary possessor." For Moore, this
affirmation of a shifting stance and perspective yields a positive pleasure, and a moral: "Too stern an intellectual emphasis upon this quality or that, detracts from one's enjoyment; / it must not wish to
disarm anything; nor may the approved triumph easily be honored—
/ that which is great because something else is small."

In the list of pictures that makes up most of the poem, the speaker affirms both that which is quotidian and middling as well as that which is peculiar and highly delineated. As an "imaginary possessor," she focuses

> upon what would give me pleasure in my average
>   moments:
> the satire upon curiosity in which no more is discernible than
> the intensity of the mood;
> or quite the opposite—the old thing, the medieval decorated
>   hat-box,
> in which there are hounds with waists diminishing like the
>   waist of the hourglass
> and deer and birds and seated people;
> it may be no more than a square of parquetry: the literal
>   biography perhaps,
> in letters standing well apart upon a parchment-like expanse;
> an artichoke in six varieties of blue; the snipe-legged
>   hieroglyphic in three parts;
> the silver fence protecting Adam's grave, or Michael taking
>   Adam by the wrist.

Importantly, then, as in all Moore's list poems, one thing is not defined in isolation but is modified through its "anthology of transit."[34] Through juxtaposition, the picture in which "no more is discernible than / the intensity of the mood," and its opposite, "the medieval decorated hat-box," are both defined *and* relativized—made peculiar *and* also middling. By grouping together "parquetry," "the letters" of a "literal biography," "artichoke," and "hieroglyphic," the spacing and patterning of these items is brought to the fore, though there is an obvious lack of equivalence between these objects. In concluding her list with a reference to Adam, Moore makes him just an item in a list of many, rather than the Adam "alone" in "In the Days of Prismatic Colour." Further, rather than associating Adam with "originality," Moore represents Adam's demise—focusing on his grave and on Michael, the guide who leads him out of paradise. Moore additionally attenuates her perspective by not focusing on Adam's angst, but rather on the silver fence protecting Adam's grave and Michael's slender hold on his wrist.

But while the form of the list quite simply, if profoundly, allows for a fluid multiplicity, Moore must still bring her poem to a close. Between the initial publication of "When I Buy Pictures" (1921) and its inclusion in her volume of verse, *Observations* (1924), Moore changed the ending three times. In *The Dial* version, Moore's excitement with her new list format leads her speaker to assert the possibility of seeing herself in a mirror, of specularity:

> It comes to this: of whatever sort it is,
> it must acknowledge the forces which have made it:
> it must be "lit with piercing glances into the life of things:"
> then I "take it in hand as a savage would take a looking-
> glass."[35]

No longer content to be an "imaginary possessor" but savagely desiring self-reflection, Moore breaks with the middling and anti-specular consciousness of her poem. Because the list provides for the possibility of fluid multiplicity, an "elsewhere," Moore paradoxically must have felt that her poetic stance was at last "firmly" established. Thus, having found a sure means of "self"-expression, she wishes the narcissistic gratification of seeing herself. In the version of this poem published in *Poems* (1921), Moore corrects for this overstatement, invoking a kind of spiritual relativity:

> It comes to this: of whatever sort it is, it
>   must make known the fact that it has been displayed
>   to acknowledge the spiritual forces which have made it;
>   and it must admit that it is the work of X, if X produced it;
>   of Y, if made
>   by Y. It must be a voluntary gift with the name written
>   on it.[36]

Avoiding the specularity of her looking glass image, Moore concludes this version of her poem by emphasizing the specificity of art objects and makers. However, for Moore this emphasis must have seemed too particular, not fluid or middling enough. In *Observations* she dropped these lines and changed the ending to:

> It comes to this: of whatever sort it is,
> it must be "lit with piercing glances into the life of things";
> it must acknowledge the spiritual forces which had made it.

While this version remains constant throughout Moore's later publications, it ends the list abruptly. Even though "lit," with its doubly directed illumination, gives the conclusion a certain ambiguity, the ending is overstated in comparison with the more subtle evocations presented earlier in the poem.

In "People's Surroundings," as in "The Labors of Hercules," Moore avoids the problem of ending her list with a singular statement by establishing a separate list within the larger one that predominates. "People's Surroundings," the last published list poem of this period, is one of Moore's most fascinating and complex poetic constructions. In the very multiplicity of the relations it sets into play, it seems to attempt to move past the format of the list to that of collage, although it returns quite decisively to the list in its visionary ending.

To attempt to make too much sense of "People's Surroundings" may be an error equal only to failing to attempt to make any sense of it. A comment about Duns Scotus, copied down by Moore in one of her notebooks (and echoed in "New York"), is suggestive for reading the poem: " 'if you enter his lists you are lost. The right way to attack him is to stand outside and laugh.' "[37] The poem might best be read from an "outside" which the poem works to establish. Toward the end of the poem, Moore writes:

> In these noncommittal, personal-impersonal expressions of
>   appearance,
> the eye knows what to skip;
> the physiognomy of conduct must not reveal the
>   skeleton;
> "a setting must not have the air of being one"
> yet with x-raylike inquisitive intensity upon it, the surfaces go
>   back;
> the interfering fringes of expression are but a stain on what
>   stands out,
> there is neither up nor down to it;

Moore urges an attention to phenomena defined by any of a number of demarcations. That is, while Moore accepts the necessity of "interfering fringes of expression"—forms of cognition which are part and parcel of seeing—she paradoxically desires her reader to see what these define and enclose, not only the definitions or boundaries themselves. Thus "People's Surroundings" advances a vision in which people are inseparable from their surroundings and in which interiors are implicated in exteriors.

Throughout "People's Surroundings" a number of determinations are mixed and matched in unconventional ways. Moore enlarges the definition of "surroundings" to include historical and psychological factors and subverts the values and associations attached to such dualities as surface and depth, and commerce and culture. In the third and fourth stanzas, the superficial "indestructible necropolis" that emerges as a distinctly American product is contrasted with the depths of a scene that exists apart from any specific historical context:

> the vast indestructible necropolis
> of composite Yawman-Erbe separable units;
> the steel, the oak, the glass, the Poor Richard publications
> containing the public secrets of efficiency
> on "paper so thin that one thousand four hundred and twenty
>   pages make one inch,"
> exclaiming so to speak, When you take my time, you take
>   something I had meant to use:
>
> the highway hid by fir trees in rhododendron twenty feet
>   deep,
> the peacocks, hand-forged gates, old Persian velvet—
> roses outlined in pale black on an ivory ground—
> the pierced iron shadows of the cedars,
> Chinese carved glass, old Waterford,
> lettered ladies; landscape gardening twisted into permanence.

Moore reverses the convention wherein a scene set within a historical context is represented as possessing temporal depth while a scene apart from its historical context is presented as a comparatively superficial picture. Furthermore, while revealing certain "superficies," or thinnesses, of American culture, Moore also reveals the depths that sustain them.[38] America contains its "public secrets of efficiency" on its own immutable and mysterious production, "paper so thin that one thousand four hundred and twenty pages make one inch." Conversely, in the following stanza, Moore urges an attention to "rhododendrons twenty feet deep," depicting objects in which depth is a

product of the surface treatment, "roses outlined in pale black on an
ivory ground." Later in the poem, Moore pairs "medicaments for instant beauty, in the hands of all" with "that live wire, the American
string quartette." The particular "live" quality of the American string
"quartette" may well have something to do with the blatantly commercial aspects of American society. Both share a quickness of hands.

John Slatin has provided a compelling and useful, if finally limited,
analysis of "People's Surroundings." Emphasizing the three-page
poem's division into two sentences (as published in *Observations*), Slatin maintains that the first sentence (of six stanzas) presents a vision
of a self-contained present without consciousness of the past, which
Moore rejects in her second sentence for a vision in which "the present belongs to the past and the past to the present":

> we see the exterior and the fundamental structure—
> captains of armies, cooks, carpenters,
> cutlers, gamesters, surgeons and armourers,
> lapidaries, silkmen, glovers, fiddlers and ballad-singers,
> sextons of churches, dyers of black cloth, hostlers and
>   chimney-sweeps,
> queens, countesses, ladies, emperors, travellers and mariners,
> dukes, princes, and gentlemen
> in their respective places—
> camps, forges and battlefields,
> conventions, oratories and wardrobes,
> dens, deserts, railway stations, asylums and places where
>   engines are made,
> shops, prisons, brickyards and altars of churches—
> in magnificent places clean and decent,
> castles, palaces, dining-halls, theatres and imperial audience
>   chambers.

However, according to Slatin, what Moore is rejecting in the first six
stanzas is not only the present of a "vast indestructible necropolis of
. . . separable units" but also the sensibilities and poetic styles of her
contemporaries. Slatin convincingly demonstrates that in the earlier
stanzas atmospheres are depicted that critique the writing of Williams, Pound, Eliot, and Stevens. For example, in the first stanza
Moore remarks:

106

they [people's surroundings] answer one's questions:
a deal table compact with the wall;
in this dried bone of arrangement,
one's "natural promptness" is compressed, not crowded out;
one's style is not lost in such simplicity.

In writing earlier of Pound, Moore referred to his "natural prompt-ness." And in a letter to Moore, Williams used the term "dried bone of arrangement" to refer to the decadence of academic rhetoric. Since Williams viewed Pound's academic leanings with dislike and suspicion, Slatin concludes that Moore is using Williams' phrase to criticize Pound indirectly while simultaneously criticizing Williams' own style as not really free of "style," despite its avowed simplicity. Slatin links the fifth stanza with an Eliot who "can like trout smell what is coming," and the sixth stanza with Stevens:

and Bluebeard's tower above the coral reefs,
the magic mousetrap closing on all points of the compass,
capping like petrified surf, the furious azure of the bay
where there is no dust and life is like a lemon-leaf,
a green piece of tough translucent parchment,
where the crimson, the copper, and the Chinese vermillion of
        the poincianas
set fire to the masonry and turquoise blues refute the clock;
this dungeon with odd notions of hospitality,
with its "chessmen carved out of moonstone,"
its mocking-birds, fringed lilies, and hibiscus,
its black butterflies with blue half circles on their wings,
tan goats with onyx ears, its lizards glittering and without
        thickness
like splashes of fire and silver on the pierced turquoise of the
        lattices
and the acacia-like lady shivering at the touch of a hand,
lost in a small collision of the orchids—
dyed quicksilver let fall
to disappear like an obedient chameleon in fiftyshades of
        mauve and amethyst:
here where the mind of this establishment has come to the
        conclusion

that it would be impossible to revolve about one's self too
    much,
sophistication has like "an escalator," "cut the nerve of
    progress."

For Slatin, who sees Moore as drawing a cameo portrait of herself in the "acacia-like lady," Moore has been undone by her "own help-lessly mimetic instincts." Realizing her own absence and the absence of other persons in the preceding stanzas, Moore corrects her vision of a dead contemporary world with a vision of an alive past. Slatin concludes: "There is no real continuity between the first and second sentences of 'People's Surroundings.' . . . . Moore writes that 'we see the exterior and the fundamental structure,' but the poem holds them so far apart that it is impossible to see them together, as we must do if we are to take seriously the possibility that the world envisioned in the final lines is immanent in and accessible to the world that occupies the first two-thirds of the poem." [39]

Provocative as it is, Slatin's interpretation fails to attend to Moore's commitment to the presentation of the surface and its present time in both parts of her poem, a commitment illustrated in poems pre-ceding and following "People's Surroundings." Furthermore, in em-phasizing her negative assessments he fails to capture Moore's ambiv-alence toward her contemporaries. While Moore may well be praising as well as faulting her peers, she may also be non-committally noting that whether she likes it or not her surroundings are the sen-sibilities and words of her contemporaries. Their writings are "people's surroundings."

Although, as Slatin notes, "the items on the concluding list are 'distinctly archaic,'" there are items which are contemporary—"rail-way stations, asylums and places where engines are made"—as, just in the preceding stanzas, there are items which evoke the past—"the pierced iron shadows of the cedars." But more importantly, Moore includes people in her last stanza, if to separate them from their sur-roundings, precisely because she has established through her preced-ing description people's presence in their surroundings. In her con-clusion, Moore flaunts the division between people and surroundings because by now she assumes that a setting does "'not have the air of being one,'" and, presumably, neither does a person.

Certainly, the concluding list emphasizes the similarities between people and surroundings. The people—both "exterior and fundamental structure"—are characterized by their roles, and the surroundings are often suggestive of specific activities that occur there. People and surroundings are joined together through functions, although they are not perfectly matched. Moore opts for the superfluity and specificity of items, rather than for their schematization. Under the aegis of the poem, the grid of the list becomes a kind of seamless web, or, as Costello remarks, "the poem seems to release words from the structures that have borne them, as if deferring to the stronger tow of dense reality."[40] Indeed, in bringing the format of the list—the structure of the poem—into prominence, Moore discloses it as a mechanism, thereby relativizing it and evading closure.

Moore is far more ambivalent about the styles of her contemporaries than Slatin suggests.[41] For example, Moore would not simply criticize Williams for possessing "style," for if she values simplicity, she also values style, commenting in a prose piece that "the man is the style."[42] And if the sixth stanza is written largely with Stevens in mind as Slatin suggests, Moore may be faulting the parts of Stevens' writing in which women and otherness are represented as transparent—"lizards glittering and without thickness"—as well as praising him for his attraction to exotic elements. Similarly, Moore's relation to the "acacia-like lady" is far from simple. While her characterization as "obedient" is unnerving in the context of a fairy-tale Bluebeard who married and then murdered his several wives, as an "obedient chameleon" the "acacia-like lady," unlike Bluebeard's wives, possesses the power to disappear at will. (In poems written before and after "People's Surroundings," Moore admires the ability of chameleons and lizards to camouflage with their environment and to appear "intermittently.")[43] And if the "acacia-like lady" is a portrait or an aspect of Moore herself, it is notable that it is at her disappearance that "the mind of this establishment" emerges; that is, if Moore is the "acacia-like lady," she is also "the mind of this establishment." And importantly, this mind does not merely condemn the sophisticated self-reflexivity of her contemporaries, as Slatin maintains, but notes rather that it has "cut the nerve of progress." Moore could not have been inattentive to the double meaning of cut—to forge as well as to sever—as she was ambivalent about "progress" itself. Moore may be at once commending self-reflexivity in that it works against a stream-lined and empty progress, and also she may be rejecting it in that its "meta" propensities break too decisively with a phenomenal reality.

In "A People's Surroundings," Moore refuses to take any side at all, establishing an expression as global and "noncommittal" as she can. Moore's poem would seem to wish to hold various sets of possibilities—surface and depth, present and past, commerce and culture, and self-reflexivity and phenomenology—in shifting and playful relations. In so doing, she is not writing a neutral or a neuter poetry in any common understanding of these terms, but is working against the over-determinations and reifications of existing thought. As a woman writer, Moore may establish her strength precisely in her capacity to imitate contemporaries, simultaneously appreciating and condemning their "styles," or her "surroundings." Indeed, in her "mimicry," in her agreeing difference, Moore produced a writing of her own "self-affection" far more significantly than if she had simply opposed her "surroundings."[44]

 "NO WEATHER SIDE":

A Sustained Achievement

The king said he liked apples,
The Queen said she liked pears,
And what shall we do to the blackbird
Who listens unawares?
      —Kate Greenaway, as quoted by Marianne Moore,
                      The Dial (1925)[1]

In what degree diverse subject-matters lend themselves
to association, is a question.
      —Marianne Moore, *The Dial* (1927)[2]

After "People's Surroundings," Moore turned from
the form of the list to collage as a means of composing an even more
far-ranging and shifting poetry. Now the contestation with language
and meaning is more subtle, as Moore extends the omniscience of
her list poems to range over items which relate to one another in
more diverse ways. Moore effects a fluid écriture in what she calls her
"hybrid method of composition" by juxtaposing phrases that have
been "said in the very best way," and thereby destablilizing and relativizing the meanings of these phrases.[3] To an even greater extent
than in her list poems, Moore establishes her stance "elsewhere" from
existing representation by her refusal to oppose or to promote any
singular attitude, thought, or expression.

Indeed, the transition from list to collage resembles the earlier
transition from contrariety to the fantastic in its movement to more
multi-faceted juxtapositions. But while in Moore's poems both of
contrariety and of the fantastic, there is a singular speaker expressing
her views (if complexly and contradictorily), in these later poems the

struggle with languages and meanings is more direct. Remarkably, up to this time in her career, Moore has pursued a rather singular path in experimenting with and discarding various poetic forms and styles in order to create a writing which, on the one hand, is made up of highly particular forms of expression and, on the other hand, is productive of unstable and shifting meanings. And while the form of collage allows Moore to produce many of her finest and certainly most complex works—including "Bowls," "Silence," "Marriage," "An Octopus," "Sea Unicorns and Land Unicorns," and "No Swan So Fine"—it is not accidental that at this time she also addresses most profoundly and directly those complicit orders of gender, representation, and thought which determine her existence as a woman and as a poet.

Collage, of course, is not Moore's invention, but first arose in the visual arts. Moore, however, through her innovative practice of quoting and footnoting, may have been instrumental in enabling this form to emerge in the literary arena. R. P. Blackmur suggests that Pound's method in *The Cantos* is derived from Moore's innovations. Pound himself, in commenting on Eliot's *Wasteland*, noted the similarity between Eliot's use of quotations and footnotes and Moore's. [4] Although Eliot's *Wasteland* predates Moore's collage poems proper, the method of collage is implicit in her earlier-established practice of quotation, and is virtually achieved in "People's Surroundings," published a few months before Eliot's poem. [5] Moore herself may have found in *The Wasteland* stimulation or permission for extending her collage method. However, regardless of the direct and indirect lines of influence between Moore and Eliot, Moore's themes and methods in her collage poems are decisively at odds with those in Eliot's *Wasteland* and may constitute a rejection of his poem. [6]

Moore's collage poems are far more ambiguous in their "agreeing difference" than Eliot's oppositional stance in *The Wasteland*. While his speaker "shores" fragments "against" his "ruin," Moore plays fragments against each other in a form of exploratory and inconclusive identity quest. Several critics have noted that Moore's quotations are less "profound" than those employed by Eliot in *The Wasteland* and Pound in *The Cantos*. Blackmur comments: "it may be observed that of all the hundreds of quotations and references in her poems, none is in itself stirring, although some are about stirring things; and in this she is

the opposite of Eliot who quotes the thing in itself stirring."[7] Kenner
remarks of Moore's notes: "[they] are not like the notes to *The Wasteland*, part of our education; we are not meant to look up the sources."[8]
While Blackmur and Kenner suggest that Moore's idiosyncratic sensibility is the reason for her election of quotations of lesser import,
her position as a woman within the culture and literary tradition
needs to be considered. She cannot and refuses to deliver her quotations from a position of cultural centrality, but rather elects to "bear"
expressions from "elsewhere." The hieratic impulses in the poetry of
Eliot and Pound, and even Stevens and Williams, are absent from
Moore's collages, for the hieratic is part of what is to be dismantled.
Indeed, Moore's juxtapositions of statements produce radical ironies
which seriously undermine the very possibility of "stirring" or "solid"
meanings. Like her description of Mount Tacoma in "An Octopus,"
her "deceptively reserved and flat" poems lie in "grandeur and mass,"
"a sea of shifting."[9]

"Snakes, Mongooses, Snake-Charmers, and the Like" and "Novices"—written just before Moore's collage poems—meditate on
qualities that the collage poems will effect. In "Snakes, Mongooses,
Snake-Charmers, and the Like," Moore imagines a "plastic animal all
of a piece." However, the poem declares, its singleness is far less compelling than what its singleness imprisons:

> one is compelled to look at it as the shadows of the alps
>   imprisoning in their folds like flies in amber, the rhythms of
>   the skating-rink.

As in Moore's earlier, list poems, there is a deliberate flaunting of
register: the large and the small, the great and the insignificant, are
duly mixed. In "Novices," Moore criticizes "the good and alive young
men," who assume overweening presences, and, like "the king, steward, and harper seated amidships" heed not "the jade and the rock
crystal" that "course about in solution." In contrast to their novice
writing, the poem urges a writing in which "action perpetuates action
and angle is at variance with angle / til submerged by the general
action" in a "drama of water against rocks." If there is to be any unity
or unification in Moore's poetry, it will not be the result of a singular

perspective imposing order on a multiplicity, but a mere illusion of unity caused by the intense drama of the interacting parts.

"Bowls," Moore's first published collage poem, is one of her most mysterious poems, and perhaps the one most disruptive of prevailing meanings. Indeed, "Bowls" has little paraphrasable meaning outside of its disclosure of qualities which are palpable and phenomenal rather than symbolic. The poem would seem motivated by impulses similar to those of Luce Irigaray's essay "The 'Mechanics' of Fluids," in which she criticizes the powerlessness of the "ruling symbolics" "to incorporate all the characteristics of nature," especially those of fluids. [10] In "Bowls," Moore similarly urges phenomenal "meanings": of a quickness that either cuts through layers or adds layers and of the contradictions between a resolute attitude and multiple, chance occurrences. The poem presents a number of incommensurate elements which when grouped together yield a multiplicity of quicknesses and layerings: a game of bowls, Chinese lacquer carving, Pompeii, one's correspondence, an etymological dictionary, and returning from "time to time to headquarters." In addition, the poem urges an appreciation of the lived textures between a resolute attitude and shifting realities—a contrast exhibited in many of Ashbery's poems. [11] One of the poem's "I"'s renounces "a policy of boorish indifference / to everything that has been said since the days of Matilda," but ironically purchases an "Etymological Dictionary of Modern English," as if despite her commitment to the present she wants to be sent as quickly and as assuredly back to the past as possible. The poem concludes with the aphorism "he who gives quickly gives twice / in nothing so much as a letter," though it suggests that the letter is destined for a publication that may well "disappear before one has time to buy it." By disclosing the qualities of palpable or phenomenal experience (including tone of voice), Moore reveals that the meanings of these experiences are not adequately represented by a meaning system in which thought is privileged over physicality. As Moore remarks in "Marriage," "We occidentals are so unemotional, we quarrel as we feed." Certainly Pound, Williams, and Stevens value physical over mental life at times, but the "meaning" of their poetry often depends on the heroics of their controversial stances, in which the side of the hierarchical dualism that is regularly devalued is elevated, causing the hierarchy to be reinscribed, if in an inverted form. Moore, on the other hand, throws wrenches into the works, disclosing meanings quite "other" than those which depend on hierarchical distinctions for their articulation.

To make meanings entirely "other" than those which are dependent on hierarchical dualities for their articulation may be to engage in lack of meaning and in silence, as a number of feminist theorists have commented.[12] Although in collage poems written after "Bowls," Moore continues to refuse conventional forms of coherence, she will enlist a number of dualities in order to utilize, if also to destabilize, their meanings. In 1923, Moore began a poetry notebook—one of the only existing, extensive records of her poetic process—which includes parts of "Silence" as well as her triptych, "Marriage," "An Octopus," and "Sea Unicorns and Land Unicorns."[13] Even though the notebook only partially develops many of the ideas and images of the poems (only "Silence" achieves a relatively stable and complete form in the notebook), it provides a telling record of Moore's "hybrid method of composition" and of the overlapping concerns of these poems—concerns with such oppositions as mystery and power, stasis and change, pacificity and violence, simplicity and complexity, solitude and companionship, femininity and masculinity, and particular entities and synthesizing wholes.

Significantly, while Moore's product is one of collage, her method of composition is vitally one of collage, as she actively mixes and remixes diverse phrases. At times in the notebooks, parts of several evolving poems are inextricably combined in passages such as the following:

> An octopus of ice
> so cool in this age of violence
> so static & so enterprising
> heightening the mystery of the medium
> the haunt of many-tailfeathers
> these rustics calling each other by their first names
> a simplification which complicates
> one says I want to be alone
> the other also I would like to be alone.
> Why not be alone together
> I have read you over all this while in silence
> silence?
> I have seen nothing in you

I have simply seen you when you were so handsome you gave
me a start

Beautiful woman—stiff with jewels
her dress embroidered all over slightly with
snakes of Venice gold & silver & some Os. [14]

The first passage contains lines from "An Octopus," "Marriage," and "Silence." In the second, lines appear from "Marriage" and "Sea Unicorns and Land Unicorns."

In initially composing her poems, Moore meditates with some frequency on the place and import of argument and logic. While the form of collage is incompatible with an underlying structure based on logic or argument, it is interesting to note that Moore, in the intermediary stages of composition, is deeply ambivalent about these. In fact, this ambivalence may well be a decisive influence in her development of a collage method. In her notebook, she criticizes marriage as an institution "deaf to argument," but is equally critical of argument: "Life is a metamorphosis not the butt of an argument / Life will at all times have its obediences but they are not obediences to argument." She writes, "sentiment emancipated is a great aid to logic / But what of that / the lack of logic is not loved and understood." Later, she notes that "the fretwork of the mind['s] great arguments have hung by very slender threads." Indeed, Moore is not willing to discard argument and logic, but she also is fearful of their possible tyranny. She seems to distrust any over-reaching explanatory system, remarking in "Marriage," "Psychology which explains everything / explains nothing." But she also fears a lack of investigation and analysis. In 1923 Moore encounters the very dilemmas currently confronting feminist artists: unwilling to consign themselves to mere critique—a critique which happens within patriarchal forms of thinking—they also recognize woman's peril within an "innocent" representation. [15]

Moore, then, at least partially circumvents this "either/or" dilemma through collage, which allows for "both/ands" and "neither/nors." By juxtaposing diverse points of view and images without hierarchizing them, Moore can disclose critical discrepancies and yet engage in celebrative ("agreeable") catalogues of existence. That is, she can simultaneously criticize and appreciate; analyze and synthesize. And in so doing, she manifests what her writing cannot and refuses to resolve—the very real contradictions that structure her writing as a woman and a poet.

In "Silence"—the shortest poem from this period—Moore simultaneously praises and criticizes a decorum of restraint, revealing the power relations that would allow some to be restrained, while condemning others to silence. Much of the interest and subtlety of the poem depends on the ways silence and restraint are contextualized and played off of one another. Typically, the poem has been interpreted as an endorsement of the father's assertion that "deepest feeling always shows itself in silence; / not in silence but in restraint." However, the poem itself is not titled "Restraint," but "Silence." And if the speaker seems to be an approving enlistee of the superior people as defined by the father, she is also a skeptical, and perhaps even bitter, observer of this father:

> My father used to say,
> "Superior people never make long visits,
> have to be shown Longfellow's grave
> nor the glass flowers at Harvard.
> Self reliant like the cat—
> that takes its prey to privacy,
> the mouse's limp tail hanging like a shoelace from its mouth—
> they sometimes enjoy solitude,
> and can be robbed of speech
> by speech which has delighted them.
> The deepest feeling always shows itself in silence;
> not in silence, but restraint."
> Nor was he insincere in saying, " 'Make my house your inn'."
> Inns are not residences.

All but two and a half lines of this poem consist of the father's pronouncement; and only at the very end of the poem does the speaker make any comment. The speaker's remarks are understated, almost to the point of inarticulateness. But because of the absence of any other comments by her, they tease the reader's desire to make sense of them. While the statement, "Inns are not residences," seems to offer a definitive judgment, it reveals very little. If the statement had been written, "Inns are not homes" or "Inns are not hotels," the nature of the speaker's comment would have been immediately clear. As it stands, the statement seems to be offered as evidence of the father's reserve and restraint, yet it also raises considerable questions about his warmth and generosity. Indeed, Moore may be presenting a patriarch whose very doctrines of self-reliance and restraint may serve to protect his own indecorous needs from other people's needs. "Make my house your inn" is taken from a biography of Edmund Burke, cited in the notes:

> "Make my house your inn": Edmund Burke to a stranger with whom he had fallen into conversation in a bookshop. Life of Burke: James Prior: "'Throw yourself into a coach', said he. 'Come down and make my house your inn.'"

Typical of Moore, the meaning of the quotation in the poem contrasts with its source. Edmund Burke's invitation is full of warmth, ease, and generosity. He seems to be saying, use my home as freely as if you were a paying guest in an inn; whereas in the father's eclipsed invitation a quite different communiqué is delivered: one is reminded that this is his house and one's access to it, and likewise to him, is limited.

Notably, then, in the father's speech, his example of self-reliance is "the cat / that takes its prey to privacy, / the mouse's limp tail hanging like a shoe lace from its mouth." Far from the Emersonian ideal of self-reliance, this example introduces issues of power into a speech ostensibly concerned with rules of decorum, which presumably should be above these bloody contingencies. As the longest line in the poem, the "limp tail hanging like a shoelace" encourages the reader to unravel the unspoken relations in "Silence."

The father's speech is further ironized if one knows that Moore never knew her father, who, unlike the upstanding patriarch represented in the poem, left the family shortly after her birth because of a nervous breakdown. In fact, the opening line, "My father used to say," and the ensuing remarks are all based on a comment made by a neighbor of Moore's, a Miss A. M. Homans, as indicated in the notes. Furthermore, Moore revised Homans' words considerably. The Miss Homans of the notes seems very concerned with following her father's instructions so that the people she visits will not regard her poorly when she is gone:

> My father used to say: a remark in conversation; Miss A. M. Homans, Professor Emeritus of Hygiene, Wellesley College. "My father used to say, 'superior people never make long visits, then people are not so glad when you've gone.' When I am visiting, I like to go about by myself. I never had to be shown Longfellow's grave nor the glass flowers at Harvard."

While Homans herself seems ruled by fear of what others will think as much as by self-reliance, Moore's speaker has greater command of herself and of her situation, coolly assessing the virtues and vices of the father's speech. In initial versions of the poem, Moore attempted to construct another character for Homans than that recorded in the notes:

> The innocuous child descendent of fearless parents
>
> Like the cat
> the only domestic animal that has not lost its wild qualities
>
> but enjoys its finds with privacy

Like the "mild wild" unicorn in "Sea Unicorns and Land Unicorns," this "innocuous child" possesses wild qualities. However, in the final version of the poem, Moore translates the quality of wildness she initially sought in the daughter's character into the speaker's restrained and ironized (wild) observations about the father. If the speaker resides in her father's house, her father's words, she does not live there completely: "Inns are not residences."

In her poem on "Silence," Moore is very restrained in speaking of the father, perhaps to escape being the victim of the father's speech—the mouse figured in the poem whose tongue is presumably "got" by the same cat. That is, certainly Moore, despite her critique of the father, does not want to do away with the practice of restraint. She clearly values its powers of communication. But neither can she simply practice the father's "restraint" because of the ways it silences her. By speaking with restraint about silence, she creates an alternative to either adherence to or rejection of the father's admonishment, refusing his delimiting either/ors. No longer compelled to pose reticence and volubility as contrarieties, Moore is powerfully voluble through her reticence—asking her reader to strain to hear the fluctuating approbation and condemnation in her concluding lines.

In "Marriage," "An Octopus," and "Sea Unicorns and Land Unicorns," Moore continues her query into the relationship between gender and forms of representation and thought. While these three poems are not strictly speaking a triptych, their shared subject matter and their proximity in Moore's volumes of verse encourage a consideration of them as a unit. In Moore's first self-edited volume of verse, *Observations* (1924), "Silence" appears after "Marriage" and before both "Octopus" and "Sea Unicorns and Land Unicorns," which conclude the volume. But in both the *Collected Poems* (1952) and the *Complete Poems* (1967), Moore grouped the three poems in an uninterrupted sequence. In the *Selected Poems* (1935), arranged by T. S. Eliot, "Novices" appears between "Marriage" and "An Octopus," and since Moore scarcely altered Eliot's arrangement of her poems in subsequent collections, her decision to place "Novices" in advance of the other three poems, keeping them together, is significant.

While writing these poems, Moore frequently referred to them jointly. Remarking in a 1924 letter to Scofield Thayer, then the editor of *The Dial*, on "An Octopus" and "Sea Unicorns and Land Unicorns," Moore commented on the poems' "recalcitrance and undesirable expansiveness, for I am most impetuous and perilously summary in anything which is to me so vital a matter."[16] In a letter written a year earlier to her brother, she criticized the just completed "Novices": "I had high hopes of it when writing but much of the nourishment had I thought been punished out of it by the time it came out."[17] Between "Novices" and these later poems, Moore seems no longer to need to "punish" their expansiveness, for the aesthetic thematized in "Novices" becomes in these later poems the principle of composition: "a precipitate of dazzling impressions" in which "action perpetuates action and angle is at variance with angle."

While no overall order can be discerned among the poems, they develop a number of interrelated thematic and representational concerns. Beginning in "Marriage" with the problem of heterosexual union, Moore in "An Octopus" and "Sea Unicorns and Land Unicorns" explores alternative conceptions of community and unity. In "Marriage," Moore implicitly criticizes a relationship of hierarchical duality in which "opposites" are "Opposed to each other, not to unity," replacing it in "An Octopus" with the natural community of Mount Tacoma and its diverse habitats and animals. In "Sea Unicorns and Land Unicorns," she turns her attention back to the problem of unities and opposites, arriving at a vision of "agreeing difference," in which "personalities by nature much opposed, / can be combined in such a way / that when they do agree, their unanimity is great." The word unanimity signals a different notion of one-ness. It is not the abstract notion of union propagated by Daniel Webster in his " 'Liberty and union / now and forever'" at the end of "Marriage," but is precisely the one-animus, the one animal, made up of four animals provisionally intertwined and not merged, so that their copulating differences of sea and land, and unicorn and lion are maintained. Indeed much of the work of the poems seems to be to destabilize and confound such hierarchical dualities as unity and diversity, depth and surface, original truth and representation, simplicity and complexity, and sublime and picturesque.

Throughout the poems, Moore moves between images of patterned surface and symbolic depth, asking her readers to attend to both simultaneously, as in the image of "Big Snow Mountain," which begins

An Octopus

Of ice. Deceptively reserved and flat,
it lies "in grandeur and in mass"
beneath a sea of shifting snow dunes:
dots of cyclamen red and maroon on its clearly defined
     pseudopodia
made of glass that will bend—a much needed invention—
comprising twenty-eight ice fields from fifty to five
     hundred feet deep
of unimagined delicacy.

While Moore's mountain possesses "grandeur and depth," it also possesses "unimagined delicacy." Similarly, images of a Romantic sublime and its obliteration of sensate experience are confounded with images of the picturesque and its visual variety:

Larkspur, blue pincushions, blue pease, and lupin;
white flower with white, and red with red;
the blue ones "growing close together
so that patches of them look like blue water in the distance";
this arrangement of colors
as in Persian designs of hard stones with enamel,
forms a pleasing equation—
a diamond outside and inside, a white dot;
on the outside, a ruby; inside, a red dot;
black spots balanced with black
in woodlands where fires have run over the ground—
separated by aspens, cats' paws, and woolly sunflowers,
fireweed, asters, and Goliath thistles
"flowering at all altitudes as multiplicitous as barley."

While the white dot and red dot may well suggest the reduction of sensate experience characteristic of the Romantic sublime, these very dots are also fine points in a patterned medley of color. The black of a fiery "sublime" destruction is simply part of a larger patterning of color.

If the three poems affirm any one principle, it is a simple complexity, rather than a complex simplicity. Part of the problem with marriage in "Marriage" is its forced simplicity, its "cycloid inclusiveness / that has dwarfed the demonstration / of Columbus with the egg." In contrast, Moore would seem to prefer the simplicity of an acknowledged complexity—the complexity of highly wrought designs, and of four animals, rather than two. For Moore there can be no simple linearity and transparent references, but only circularity and opaque references, since she does not possess a singular, centered relation to the literary tradition and larger representational orders.[18] "Marriage" itself is "bright" with "circular traditions." In "An Octopus," "Completing a circle, / you have been deceived into thinking that you have progressed." Appropriately, "Sea Unicorns and Land Unicorns" with its quadrupling complexity of "agreeing difference" does not offer an absolute rebuttal to a marriage of opposites, but concludes with an erased version of the Adam and Eve in the unicorn and lady, "both curiously wild and gentle."

In the opening lines of "Marriage," Moore initiates a manner of writing which signals that she cannot and will not offer any transparent insights or singular conclusions:

> This institution
> perhaps one should say enterprise
> out of respect for which
> one says one need not change one's mind
> about a thing one has believed in,
> requiring public promises
> of one's intention
> to fulfill a private obligation

The syntax is deliberately convoluted. The opening is more readable if the relative clause, "which / one says one need not change one's mind / about," is repositioned: This institution, perhaps one should say enterprise out of respect for a thing, about which one says one need not change one's mind, requiring public promises of one's intention to fulfill a private obligation. Although this version is clumsy, these lines begin to make sense—the "about" placed by Moore at the end of the clause providing the clue for the changed order. Keeping her readers from any transparent reading, Moore seems to be repudiating the very possibility of a singular viewpoint on marriage. Even with the clarified syntax above, the sentence remains ambiguous with respect to who need not change one's mind: the speaker or the marrieds. And is it good not to have to change one's mind or is it the unfortunate by-product of the institutional nature of the relationship? In addition, by labeling marriage "this institution / perhaps . . . enterprise," Moore invites her readers to consider multiple aspects of marriage as revealed through the positive and negative connotations of these key terms. As an institution, marriage is enduring, yet also staid; and as an enterprise, marriage is based on certain economic realities, yet also inspires human energies. In referring to marriage as requiring "public promises" and "private obligations," Moore further mixes positive and negative associations. Indeed, Moore's "public promises" and "private obligations" seem to have gotten it all wrong, making public what should be privately cherished and making private what should be publicly revealed. In a discarded earlier version, this poem began:

this institution shall one say enterprise
with catfish mouth
so wide it is in danger of turning inside out.

Certainly, Moore must open her mouth very wide to speak the "inside out" of this institution, which while it inspires very real human energies—energies Moore values—it also condemns women and men to "impostures," and requires "all one's criminal ingenuity / to avoid!"

Although Moore is intrigued by this institution/enterprise that is more than she can express it to be, and is appreciative of certain aspects of it, "Marriage" forms a powerful critique of this central institution of patriarchy and of male and female roles within it.[19] While this poem discloses the imbalance of power between men and women within marriage, it also establishes the forms of thinking and representation that make this imbalance possible: "that striking grasp of opposites / opposed each to the other, not to unity." While the few critics who have considered "Marriage" at any length typically have sought to sort out blame between Adam and Eve, such an approach misses the accomplishment of Moore's meditation on marriage as a "cycloid inclusiveness" in which the parts are defined by their relationship to each other.[20] If in many ways Moore is attracted to the non-sense of Marriage, she abhors its ill-reason—the occlusion of otherness by a forced and unreasoned unity. Moore, like Irigaray and others, is criticizing a hierarchical duality in which a privileged term absorbs the otherness of the secondary term under an ideal of unity or identity (of "the same"). Adam, as the privileged term, "loves himself so much, / he can permit himself / no rival in that love"; and Eve, as the suppressed term, "loves herself so much, / she cannot see herself enough." As egotist and narcissist, they are condemned to solitary confinement within an institution which, while based on their sexual difference, will not admit to any actual otherness.

The central myth around which "Marriage" forms is the story of Adam and Eve—the Adam and Eve, at least in part, of Milton's *Paradise Lost*. Although Moore conveys the grandeur and splendor of Milton's *Paradise Lost* in passages such as "Below the incandescent stars / below the incandescent fruit, / the strange experience of beauty; / its existence is too much," she also parodies his tragic argument—absorbing and deploying its epic grandeur. Milton affirms the hierarchical order by describing Eve as "for Adam and the God in him," and in the passage in which Eve addresses Adam: "O thou for whom / And from whom I was form'd flesh of thy flesh, / And without whom am to no end, my Guide / and Head."[21] Moore subverts that hierarchy by introducing Eve into her poem first and referring to Adam as the visitor. Moore also converts Eve's respectful address into a comic epithet: "the O thou / to whom, from whom, / without whom nothing—Adam." She further subverts the Biblical and Miltonic versions of the story by providing Adam and Eve each with their own respective source of temptation: Hera's golden apples in the Hesperides and the snake. In neither case is the agony of temptation emphasized. Adam is quite simply bedazzled by the apple, "the illusion of a fire / effectual to extinguish fire," and Eve's relation to the snake is described as "that invaluable accident / exonerating Adam."

But if differences exist between Moore's and Milton's poems, Moore also borrows, and builds on, certain characteristics of Milton's Adam and Eve. Both Milton's and Moore's Adams possess language innately. In *Paradise Lost*, just after Adam's creation, he awakes to find himself endowed preternaturally with language:

> But who I was or where, or from what cause,
> Knew not; to speak I tri'd, and forthwith spake,
> My tongue obey'd and readily could name
> Whate'er I saw.[22]

Moore's Adam is blessed with the same immediate access to language, albeit comically:

> Alive with words,
> vibrating like a cymbal
> touched before it has been struck

Both Milton and Moore portray Eve as narcissistic. Milton's Eve describes her awakening from creation to Adam thus:

> The day I oft remember, when from sleep
> I first awak't, and found myself repos'd
> Under a shade on flow'rs, much wond'ring where
> And what I was, whence thither brought, and how,
> Not distant far from thence a murmuring sound

Of waters issue'd from a Cave and spread
Into a liquid Plain, then stood unmov'd
Pure as th' expanse of Heav'n; I thither went
With unexperienc't thought, and laid me down
On the green bank, to look into the clear
Smooth Lake, that to me seem'd another Sky.
As I bent down to look, just opposite,
A Shape within the wat'ry gleam appear'd
Bending to look on me, I started back,
It started back, but pleas'd I soon return'd,
Pleas'd it returned as soon with answering looks
Of sympathy and love: there I had fixt
Mine eyes till now, and pin'd with vain desire,
Had not a voice thus warned me, What thou seest,
What there thou seest fair Creature is thyself
With thee it came and goes: but follow me . . .
                              what could I do,
But follow straight, invisibly thus led?
Till I espied thee fair indeed and tall,
Under a Platan, yet methought less fair,
Less winning soft, less amiably mild
Than that smooth wat'ry image; back I turned.[23]

Emphasizing Eve's narcissistic qualities—"she cannot see herself
enough"—Moore also portrays her as possessing an non-Adamic relation to language:

> able to write simultaneously
> in three languages—
> English, German and French
> and talk in the meantime;
> equally positive in demanding a commotion
> and in stipulating quiet.

Eve's relationship to language is characterized by multiplicity. In fact,
she may not be able to see herself enough because, unlike Adam, she
does not possess a specular relation to language. According to Irigaray, women cannot be truly narcissistic, for their relation to language precludes a true narcissism. Consequently they come nearest

to a language of their own self-affection when they engage in a con-. tradictory or multiple expression, an écriture.

Although Moore disclaims psychology at the beginning of "Marriage," this poem nonetheless espouses a different kind of psychology than the dominant Freudian psychoanalysis of her day. For Moore, as for Irigaray, women's psychology is inseparable from the "place" of women within socially constructed meanings. Adam, before marriage, possesses the "ease of a philosopher unfathered by a woman"; Eve is "the logical last touch / earned as wages for work done." Appropriately, when Adam, who finds positive definition within a specular discourse, turns his attention to women, he experiences them as the absence, death, and silence to which his language condemns them:

> He says, "These mummies
> must be handled carefully—
> 'the crumbs from a lion's meal,
> a couple of shins and the bit of an ear';
> turn to the letter M
> and you will find
> that 'a wife is a coffin,'"
> that severe object
> with the pleasing geometry
> stipulating space and not people,
> refusing to be buried
> and uniquely disappointing,
> revengefully wrought in the attitude
> of an adoring child
> to a distinguished parent."

Earlier in "Marriage," Adam is plagued by the silence of the nightingale—"not its silence, but its silences." He is frustrated by his inability to make the bird sing for him:

> "He dares not clap his hands
> to make it go on
> lest it should fly off;
> if he does nothing it will sleep;
> if he cries out it will not understand."

127

The plurality of the nightingale's silences links it to the plurality of Eve's speech. And in this poem of multiple allusions to Greek myth—Hymen, Hercules, Hesperides, Diana—it also powerfully recalls the myth of the rape of Philomela by her sister's husband, Tereus. Although Tereus cuts out her tongue, Philomela succeeds in communicating her story to her sister, Procne, by weaving it into a robe. As revenge, Procne serves up their son to Tereus for dinner. Realizing what has happened, Tereus pursues the sisters who, running, are turned into a swallow and a nightingale. [24] While Moore makes no specific allusion to the Philomela story and does not connect the nightingale's silence in her poem to any act of violence, it would be entirely characteristic of her to refer to Philomela's violation and silencing by secreting and thereby mimicking the myth in her poem.

Moore's description of Adam's frustrated inability to make the bird sing for him is taken from Edward Thomas' *Feminine Influence on the Poets.* [25] But as is frequently the case, Moore has reversed the tenor of the quotation. In Thomas, who is analyzing the significance of the presence of the nightingale in "The King is Quair" by King James the First of Scotland, the nightingale is a companion-substitute for the "golden-haired maiden" desired by the king. On the cessation of the nightingale's singing, Thomas conveys the king's longing for the beauty of the song; Moore emphasizes Adam's frustration, his being "unnerved" and "plagued." Thomas extols:

> To us the central experience is everything—the strong, unhappy king, looking out of the prison window and seeing the golden-haired maiden in rich attire trimmed with pearls, rubies, emeralds, and sapphires, a chaplet of red, white and blue feathers on her head, a heart-shaped ruby on a chain of fine gold hanging over her white throat, her dress looped up carelessly to walk in that fresh morning of nightingales in the new-leaved thickets—she in her youth, loveliness and meek carriage, and her little dog with his bells to be envied because he plays at her side. The nightingale stops singing. He dares not clap his hands to make it go on lest it should fly off; if he does nothing it will sleep: if he calls out it will not understand; and he begs the wind to shake the leaves and awake the song.

In Moore's quotation of this passage in her "Notes," she eliminates Thomas' chauvinistic effusions, while purporting to quote him directly. Gone from Thomas' words is the phrase "youth, loveliness and meek carriage," and the king's envy of the dog "because he plays at her side." In *Feminine Influence on the Poets*, Thomas quite rightly describes the centrality of women's place in the (male) lyric poetic tradition. In "Marriage," Moore notes the empty "silence" of that place for women, and emphasizes the man's frustrated possessiveness rather than the pathos of his longing.

If Adam experiences Eve as absence and silence, Eve views Adam as too simply identified with the products of his own value system:

> " 'Men are monopolists
> of stars, garters, buttons
> and other shining baubles'—
> unfit to be the guardians
> of another person's happiness."

These lines represent a deliberate misuse of a quotation from a speech by Carey Thomas, President Emeritus of Bryn Mawr College:

> Men practically reserve for themselves stately funerals, splendid monuments, memorial statues, membership in academies, medals, titles, honorary degrees, stars, garters, ribbons, buttons and other shining baubles, so valueless in themselves and yet so infinitely desirable because they are symbols of recognition by their fellow craftsmen of difficult work well done."

Carey Thomas emphasizes the symbolic value of what would otherwise be baubles. Moore stresses that the attachment to symbols of one's worth degenerates into a desire to possess baubles.

Although Moore presents a comic vision of misalignment between Adam and Eve, she cannot conclude her poem in the traditional manner of comedy (with a marriage) and remain true to her vision. Instead, Moore elects to mimic the pacing and tone of a grande finale while she continues to disclose critical discrepancies between expectation and actuality, effort and result, and rhetoric and reality. Confronted at this time in her life with the marriages of her friend Bryher and of her brother, as well as possibly a proposal of marriage, perhaps what Moore may most fear about marriage is its "simplicity of temper."[26] For if Moore is enticed by marriage's circular nonsense, she is repulsed by its unremitting "malaria."

As she initiates the conclusion of her poem with the question, "What can one do for them"—these marrieds—she seems to conclude—not much—as each subsequent assertion bears counter witness to itself in an open fire of language unchecked by language:

> What can one do for them—
> these savages
> condemned to disaffect
> all those who are not visionaries
> alert to undertake the silly task
> of making people noble?
> This model of petrine fidelity
> who "leaves her peaceful husband
> only because she has seen enough of him"—
> that orator reminding you,
> "I am yours to command."
> "Everything to do with love is mystery;
> it is more than a day's work
> to investigate this science."

These lines are compelling because they reveal how fervently held beliefs contain the basis for their reversal. For example, it is precisely because the wife is a "model of petrine [Peter-like] fidelity" that she can leave her husband so simply; and because her husband orates, "I am yours to command," that he means nothing of the kind. The point of view here, as it is throughout this poem and much of Moore's work, is at times so elusive and subtle as to escape analysis. It resembles the point of view in many of Virginia Woolf's novels, in which perspective imperceptibly shifts between authorial and character consciousness, creating a hybrid consciousness. Thus, while the speaker seems to be asking the initial question in the passage quoted above, she picks up shades of meaning from those married to whom the question is addressed. Quite simply, the speaker is mocking the idea that marriage makes people noble. But she extends her parody by exposing the language of these visionaries who, in their exasperation at those who believe differently than they, might say that to do so is "silly." However, their very choice of language betrays their own cause, for if it is silly not to marry, it cannot be so visionary to marry, and the visionary pretences might indeed be a little silly.

To this already "catfish mouth" ending, Moore adds a thirty-one-

line sentence—a parody of a grande finale by which a poem celebrating the triumph of marriage might end. While the conclusion
continues to disclose the hidden contradictions in simple speech
acts, it more explicitly focuses attention on forced resolutions which
parade as eloquent truths:

> One sees that it is rare—
> that striking grasp of opposites
> opposed each to the other, not to unity,
> which in cycloid inclusiveness
> has dwarfed the demonstration
> of Columbus with the egg—
> a triumph of simplicity—
> that charitive Euroclydon
> of frightening disinterestedness
> which the world hates,
> admitting:

>> "I am such a cow,
>> if I had a sorrow,
>> I should feel it a long time:
>> I am not one of those
>> who have a great sorrow
>> in the morning
>> and a great joy at noon;"

> which says: "I have encountered it
> among those unpretentious
> protegés of wisdom
> where seeming to parade
> as the debater and the Roman,
> the statesmanship
> of an archaic Daniel Webster
> persists to their simplicity of temper
> as the essence of the matter:

>> 'Liberty and union
>> now and forever;'

the book on the writing-table;
the hand in the breast-pocket."

In extolling marriage's "cycloid inclusiveness" as having "dwarfed the demonstration / of Columbus with the egg," Moore evokes the mixed response of laughter and irritation when a complex problem is solved merely by changing registers, revealing the destructiveness of one who would force resolutions despite the problem at hand. (Columbus, boasting that he could make an egg stand up, made good on his claim by breaking an end of it, and flattening it.) The speech "I am such a cow" contains its own counter-confession: on the one hand, the making public of one's depth of emotion through a comparison to an animal of longstanding, as it were, reveals a simple-mindedness and trust (qualities productive of emotional fidelity), but, on the other hand, may be a vacuous braying, or mooing. The juxtaposition of this speech with Daniel Webster's self-contradictory "'Liberty and union / now and forever,' " further undercuts both speeches. While the first speech is plain and concrete and the second speech is dignified and abstract, both suggest a "simplicity of temper" that hides a battlefield of contradictions. The concluding images—"book on the writing-table" and "hand in the breast pocket"—are evocative of ceremonies of marriage, judiciary, and state. But in a ceremony of state, presumably the hand should be patriotically *outside* the breast pocket, or in a ceremony of the court, the hand should be *on* the book. Only in a wedding ceremony might the hand be in the pocket and the book on the table. But Webster could be reaching for just about anything—a ring, a wallet, or a gun. But even if Webster is performing the honorable actions of a wedding ceremony, his behavior is cast into suspicion by other, dishonorable possibilities. And, if there is any one lesson taught in Moore's poem, it is that marriage's pretenses to sincerity and simplicity only intensify its bottled-up lies and contradictions.

After taking on the formidable subject of "Marriage," Moore turns her attention to the sublime "Big Snow Mountain" in "An Octopus." Rejecting in "Marriage" notions of unity and community in which a "cycloid inclusiveness" compromises the parts, Moore in "An Octopus" celebrates the diversity of creatures and plants that make up the natural, found community of Mount Tacoma. Appropriately, the underlying "rock" of the mountain is "recognised by its plants and animals" and "seems frail" compared to the "dark energy of life" of the multiplicitous "fir trees." Investigating established social orders in "Marriage," Moore portrays a largely three-dimensional world, but considering the utopian community of the mountain in "An Octopus," she frequently engages a two-dimensional seeing. Thus, in "Marriage," an "industrious waterfall," a "speedy stream which violently bears all before it," conforms to the law of gravity; whereas in "An Octopus," in the flattened "perspective of the peaks," "the waterfall . . . never seems to fall—/ an endless skein swayed by the wind, / immune to the force of gravity."

As a poem which studies and celebrates local rather than general conditions, "An Octopus" not only meditates on the diversity of Mount Tacoma, but playfully seeks to locate its own properties there. The poem consists of twenty-eight sentences, corresponding in number to the mountain's twenty-eight ice fields.[27] And like the "tightly wattled spruce twigs / 'conformed to an edge like clipped cypress,'" the poem practices and celebrates "Neatness of finish! Neatness of finish!" For Moore, then, "neatness of finish" is not an inclusive closure, "a cycloid inclusiveness," but the firmly kept edge that separates each of her particular apprehensions. The qualities she praises as the "nature of this octopus" are the same qualities she strives to attain in her collage poetry: "Relentless accuracy," "capacity for fact," and "approach from all directions."

For Moore, the mountain is important not only as a natural phenomenon, but for the languages, myths, and cultures associated with it. Nearly two-thirds of the lines can be accounted for by reference to various sources.[28] Prominent among them are books by naturalists and "government pamphleteers on our natural parks." As in "Poetry," Moore is fascinated by the "poetry" of the "un-poetic" languages of officialdom. In fact, she prefers the vigor and quirky understatement of the park rules and regulations over the remote wisdom of the Greeks. Dismissing the Greeks, she writes:

> "Emotionally sensitive, their hearts were hard";
> their wisdom was remote
> from that of these odd oracles of cool official sarcasm
> upon this game preserve
> where "guns, nets, seines, traps and explosives,
> hired vehicles, gambling and intoxicants are prohibited,

disobedient persons being summarily removed
and not allowed to return without permission in writing."

For Moore, as for John Ashbery, un-poetic uses of language create
atmospheric enclaves as palpably present as their referents.

The presence of Moore's prolonged meditation on the Greeks in
"An Octopus" has puzzled many readers. It is less puzzling if one
considers that Moore may be attempting simultaneously to call up
and erase images of the old world's "Big Snow Mountain"—Mount
Olympus. Moore criticizes Greek thought which resolves "with benevolent conclusiveness, / 'complexities which still will be complexities / as long as the world lasts.'" Instead, Moore upholds the inter-
action of mind and environment, finding in the multifaceted forest
the stimulus for an "eloquent" material production:

> Bows, arrows, oars, and paddles for which trees provide the
> wood,
> in new countries are more eloquent than elsewhere—
> augmenting evidence for the assertion
> that essentially humane,
> "the forest affords wood for dwellings and by its beauty
> stimulates
> the moral vigor of its citizens."

Moore would seem to subscribe neither exclusively to simple refer-
entiality in language nor to self-referentiality, maintaining a dynamic
perspective in which both are operative: a sense of language and culture as at once determined by and determining an external realm.

On "Big Snow Mountain," only one couple is mentioned, Calypso
and her "principal," not exclusive, companion—bluejay. The inclusion of this couple in a scene in which no other entities are portrayed
as paired may well be a comic deconstruction of the serious attention
given to Adam and Eve in "Marriage." (In Moore's notebook, references to Adam and Eve are mixed in with her descriptions of paradis-
ical Mount Tacoma.) The mountain is portrayed as a haven for feminine presences:

> Inimical to "bristling, puny, swearing men
> equipped with saws and axes,"
> this treacherous glass mountain

admires gentians, ladyslippers, harebells, mountain dryads,
and "Calypso, the goat flower—
that greenish orchid fond of snow"—
anomalously nourished upon shelving glacial ledges
where climbers have not gone or have gone timidly,
"the one resting his nerves while the other advanced,"
on this volcano with the bluejay, her principal companion.
"Hopping stiffly on sharp feet" like miniature icehacks—
"secretive, with a lack of wisdom and distinction, but a villain
fond of human society or the crumbs that go with it"

Like Eve, Calypso is associated with surfaces that can mirror, and like Adam, bluejay is eager for the crumbs of society—the "stars, garters, buttons / and other shining baubles" noted in "Marriage." However, unlike Adam, bluejay does not revere himself, making an appealing, if villainous, appearance beside Calypso. And unlike Eve, "who cannot see herself enough," Calypso does not attempt to feed on her own image, but is "anomalously nourished upon shelving glacial ledges." Calypso and bluejay, representatives respectively of the mythic and natural realms, are entirely "other" from each other. Yet their relationship seems to exist comfortably within, or perhaps because of, these differences.

Moore concludes "An Octopus" through a kind of deus ex machina, foregrounding the fictionality of her poem. As much as Moore extols the mountain as a natural phenomenon, she also wishes to signal the fictional moment of her own writing; its "neatness of finish" depends on this "relentless accuracy:"

Is tree the word for these strange things
"flat on the ground like vines":
some "bent in a half circle with branches on one side
suggesting dustbrushes, not trees;
some finding strength in union, forming little stunted groves,
their flattened mats of branches shrunk in trying to escape"
from the hard mountain "planed by ice and polished by the
        wind"—
the white volcano with no weather side;
the lightning flashing at its base,
rain falling in the valleys, and snow falling on the peak—

the glassy octopus symmetrically pointed,
its claw cut by the avalanche
"with a sound like the crack of a rifle,
in a curtain of powdered snow launched like a waterfall."

Although in ending her poem Moore creates a decidedly sublime image of the mountain, its sublimity is constituted through such picturesque elements as trees that appear like "dustbrushes," and is disclosed as fictional. With the "crack of a rifle" (possibly Webster's gun at last going off) and the falling of "a curtain," Moore theatrically concludes "An Octopus."

While "An Octopus" allowed Moore to affirm and celebrate a community which is not based on the marriage contract, she was not content to rest her meditation on the complicit orders of gender, representation, and thought solely on her exposé of this natural, found community. In "Sea Unicorns and Land Unicorns," Moore reapproaches questions of coupled opposites and unity. In this poem, the specifically gendered nature of the opposites is erased, and a foursome of sea and land unicorns, and sea and land lions creates an excess of possible copulations. The new world mirrors Britain's land lions and sea unicorns with a difference—in the new world sea lions sport with land unicorns. The abstract notion of unity in "Marriage"—"'Liberty and union / now and forever'"—is replaced by an animated unanimity in which "personalities by nature much opposed, / can be combined in such a way / that when they do agree, their unanimity is great." Whereas in "Marriage" unity is forever, in "Sea Unicorns and Land Unicorns" unanimity is provisional. In conceiving the four animals as embroidered with entwined flowers and greenery, Moore emphasizes the diverse "threads" which compose their unanimity:

You have remarked this fourfold combination of strange
        animals,
upon embroideries
enwrought with "polished garlands" of agreeing difference—
thorns, "myrtle rods, and shafts of bay,"
"cobwebs, and knotts, and mulberries"
of lapis-lazuli and pomegranate and malachite[29]

Importantly, the four animals are portrayed in a relationship of reciprocity. In her quadrupled mirroring, there can be no "denigration of female difference into otherness without reciprocity".[30]

> the lion standing up against this screen of woven air
> which is the forest:
> the unicorn also, on its hind legs in reciprocity.

And while the lions and unicorns remain opposites of a kind, their qualities defy conventional hierarchical dualities. The lion is "civilly rampant" and "tame and concessive"; the unicorn is "mild wild" and "miraculous" and "elusive." While the lion is allied with given domestic and civil orders and the unicorn is seen as outside these orders (as are respectively Moore's males and females in the preceding poems), Moore subverts the far more conventional associations of maleness with the public realm and wildness, and femaleness with domesticity and tameness.

"Sea Unicorns and Land Unicorns," in fact, offers two ideal visions. In the first part of the poem the ideal of "agreeing difference," of a fourfold reciprocity, is presented. In the second part, Moore portrays the ideal of a voluntary and reciprocal meeting between the "mild wild" unicorn and the "lady inoffensive like itself." While the fourfold combinations of strange animals would seem largely to evade gender hierarchies, Moore's specific characterizations of her lions and unicorns and lady reinvokes them, if to represent them differently. Indeed, the poem seems torn between erasing gender distinctions and celebrating a specifically feminine preeminence, though it manifests little tension as Moore slips from her ideal of reciprocating lion and unicorn to her meditation on the unicorn and the lady. This transition is possible because Moore, having imagined an ideal of reciprocating otherness, can consider the relation of maiden and unicorn not as "opposites / opposed each to the other"—as the phallic unicorn and the maiden are traditionally represented—but as entities which are both similar *and* different.

Indeed, by initially conceiving of four rather than two as a basic existential structure, Moore may be approaching a constitutive moment of identity formation. In Lacan's mirror stage, the moment in which identity is established can quadruple. Jan Montefiore, in *Feminism and Poetry*, comments on this multiplication:

> the mother at once "grants the baby an image" and "deflects it," because although her look (and perhaps smile) are seen in the mirror by the baby at the same time as its own image, her presence is "split" in the same ways as the child, who must connect the feeling of her embrace with its visual counterpart (her mirror-image), and must likewise negotiate the gap between the body's feeling of being contained and the mind's identification with the visual image. The image is thus multiplied or, more accurately, quadrupled, as two pairs (one seen and one felt) of babies and of mothers."[31]

Indeed, Moore, who maintained an extremely close relationship to her mother throughout much of her life, may be attempting to call up structures of identity formation in an effort to come to terms with her own representational and life crises. And as such theorists as Irigaray, as well as Margaret Homans and Julia Kristeva, have suggested, women may well seek to locate a sense of themselves apart from their compromised position within a symbolic or specular language through their recollections of a pre-symbolic relationship to the mother. In remembering or establishing the lack of a singular identity in "identity" formations, Moore rejects the very basis for cultural forms of exclusivity—those either/ors which allow virgins to be represented in singular opposition to phallic unicorns.

One fascinating aspect of "Sea Unicorns and Land Unicorns" is the texture created through its renderings of seemingly two-dimensional and three-dimensional realities, of reproductions and unfettered originals, and of fantastical and natural forms. As in other passages in the poem, the conclusion invokes various representational possibilities in an edgy whole, repudiating the very possibility of a "smoothness" which has no hidden "back":

> Upon the printed page,
> also by word of mouth,
> we have a record of it all
> and how, unfearful of deceit,
> etched like an equine monster on an old celestial map,
> beside a cloud or dress of Virgin-Mary blue,
> improved "all over slightly with snakes of Venice gold,

and silver, and some O's,"
the unicorn "with pavon high," approaches eagerly,
until engrossed by what appears of this strange enemy,
upon the map, "upon her lap,"
its "mild wild head doth lie."

From "Marriage" to "Sea Unicorns and Land Unicorns," Moore has moved from a critique of marriage and "opposed opposites" to an affirmative vision of "agreeing difference" and of a "reciprocated femininity." Increasingly inserting two-dimensional and fictional representations into her triptych, Moore urges attention to the constructed, made-up quality of reality. And, through her conceptions of community, as defined by its diversity of creatures, habitats, and languages, and of unity as unanimity, Moore envisions social orders that actualize the "elsewhere" from which she has been writing all along.

6 / "OVERSTATEMENT":

The Later Poems and a Diminished Vision

There are, on the other hand, a few books that I still keep on my desk, and a great number that I shall never open again. But the books that a man needs to know in order to "get his bearings," in order to have a sound judgment of any bit of writing that may come before him, are very few.

—Ezra Pound, *New York Herald Tribune* (1929)[1]

When an artist is willing that the expressiveness of his work be overlooked by any but those who are interested enough to find it, he has freedom in which to realize without interference, conceptions which he personally values. But advertising, the opposite of such intensiveness, has its uses. . . . The semi-confidential impartial enthusiasm of the pre-auction descriptive catalogue suggests a desirable mechanics of eulogy and the same kind of honor without exaggeration is seen occasionally in guide books and travel bureau advertisements.

—Marianne Moore, *The Dial* (1929)[2]

From the point of view of Moore's poetry, it is perhaps a great misfortune that at this time in her life she was offered, and accepted, the demanding editorship of *The Dial*. Serving as editor from 1925–29, Moore didn't publish any additional poetry until 1932—a hiatus of more than seven years. When she again appeared in literary magazines with her new poems, she had already begun to leave behind the more radical and comprehensive concerns addressed in her earlier work. Although a few of her poems from the 1930's, such as "The Plumet Basilisk" and "No Swan So Fine," attain the excellence of her earlier verse, the later poetry is by comparison largely disappointing.[3]

In her later poetry, Moore relinquishes her paradoxical quest—to construct a universal consciousness out of a "direct treatment of the 'thing'" and to write a universal poetry which includes her perspective as a woman. From a poetry of understatement and inconclusive encounters with the larger literary tradition and system of representation, Moore begins to compose a poetry of overstatement and positive assertion of values. While her earlier poetry enunciates Moore's difference from dominant cultural meanings, her later poetry largely capitulates to them. For the first extended time in her poetic career, Moore promotes only one side of a proposition, writing a poetry of thematic and symbolic unity. Indeed, Moore re-enlists many of the hierarchical dualisms carefully subverted in her earlier poetry, frequently promoting the conventionally privileged or valued term.

Marie Borroff, in a close stylistic and rhetorical anaysis of several of Moore's later poems, has used the term "promotional prose" to describe many of Moore's most pronounced poetic effects.[4] Although Borroff provides very different reasons for Moore's rhetorical and stylistic strategies than I do, her description of Moore's later poetry is very useful.[5] Designating as "promotional prose" journalistic feature articles as well as advertisements, Borroff comments:

> The staple of the feature article is "the remarkable" in all its forms: it regales us with accounts of preeminence in performance and endurance, describes the amazing feats of animals, birds, and insects, caters to our curiosity about the genius or champion in every field of human endeavor. . . . The world as portrayed for us by the feature article is not so much idealized and exalted as it is brightened and heightened, with a kind of "Believe-It-or-Not" vividness surpassing the qualities of everyday experience.

In drawing a parallel between the stylistic and rhetorical devices of promotional prose and Moore's poetry, Borroff notes that neither is comprehensive nor pretentious. Further,

> the unpretentiousness of the feature article extends to its author as the expounding "I" through the medium of whose words its content reaches us. This author may tell us about someone who is famous, but we do not expect him to be famous himself; indeed, we pay little if any heed to him as a personality in his own right.

Indeed, Moore's later poetry is neither comprehensive nor pretentious, for she is no longer engaged in the paradoxical quest of attempting to construct a universal consciousness out of a "direct treatment of the 'thing,'" or to write a universal poetry which includes her perspective as a woman. As a writer of promotional prose, Moore may appear to be writing as a representative of her culture, but this poetry is actually predicated on her disappearance. Moore, as a woman, can recommend aspects of her culture, but she cannot represent it. And as the consciousness of her poetry shifts from an implied "I" to an implied "we," Moore's own unrepresentable needs and desires disappear, no longer informing her poetry.

The reasons for this change in Moore's poetry are most likely multiple and extra-literary (as well as literary), and could easily be the focus for an entire book-length critical biography on Moore, so remarkable is the transformation. Moore's position as editor of *The Dial* may have directed her concentration away from her own reactions, thereby confusing her initial sensibility based on her sense of alienation from dominant cultural meanings. Furthermore, as an increasingly prominent literary figure, Moore's own needs and desires may have shifted. As a recognized woman of letters, Moore may not have been able to summon up her earlier questions about poetry, for they were partly, if inadequately, answered by her own accession to the public role of poet and literary critic. As an unrecognized woman poet, Moore could not presume to be a universal representative of her culture, but as a publicly sanctioned woman poet she gained the authority to promote aspects of her culture—if not to represent it.

In addition, as Moore faced a variety of personal and public crises in the 1930's and 1940's, her understated and decentered poetry may have seemed insufficient to her. Moore was well aware that her poetry did not always communicate to those closest to her, much less to a larger, more diverse public.[6] Moreover, she may have needed to establish firmer stances in order to negotiate an increasingly troubling world and life. Such major public events as the Depression and the threat and actuality of World War II preoccupied Moore and inculcated a political conservatism.[7] In addition, throughout this period both she and her mother were afflicted by illnesses, which culminated in the decrepitude and death of her mother in 1947. Certainly the fear of losing and then the loss of her primary life companion, who was also "the first reader, collaborator . . . and critic" of her verse, severely affected Moore.[8] David Kalstone, in his critical biography of Elizabeth Bishop, comments:

> One day we may know the full details of Moore's sufferings in the 1940's. Between her own illnesses and her mother's she was growing more and more desperate. . . . In 1946 and 1947 . . . Moore's handwriting grew smaller and smaller, until finally in the letter she wrote to announce her mother's death to Bishop, it suddenly exploded into over-size characters.[9]

Although Mary Warner Moore was not always enthusiastic about her daughter's poetry, criticizing it as oblique and ephemeral, and discounting at times poetry itself as a serious endeavor, Moore wrote early in the 1950's of her mother: "The thing must be admitted, I don't care for the books that were not worked on by her."[10] Indeed, the increasingly homiletic and pious voice of Moore's poems just before and after her mother's death may well be an attempt to keep her mother's presence alive in her poetry.[11]

Even as early as 1937, Moore can be seen to be decisively taking on her mother's judgments and values. In a remarkable letter to Elizabeth Bishop, Moore corrects Bishop's writing in a manner highly reminiscent of Moore's mother's comments on Moore's writing while she was at Bryn Mawr: "When I set out to find fault with you, there are so many excellencies in your mechanics that I seem to be commending you instead, and I wish to say above all, that I am sure good treatment is a handicap unless along with it, significant values come with an essential baldness."[12] In 1908, Moore's mother condemned Moore's work for not evincing the right kind of religious values. But, at this time in her life, Moore upheld the validity of her own "distracting influences": "Ruth writes better and thinks better than I but that she 'feels' better I am not willing to confess. . . . She is mature in method and attitude and so on, but not 'susceptible' as far as I know to distracting influences, devils, wildness, and so on."[13]

Moore's later poetry records her change in direction and at times a sense of defeat, if also an elected and necessary resignation. In her early poem, "Black Earth" (1918), also titled "Melancthon," Moore upholds the "unreason" of the elephant: "Will / depth be depth, thick skin be thick, to no one who can see no / beautiful element of unreason under it?"[14] But in her 1943 poem, "Elephants," she describes an entirely different animal: "With trunk tucked up compactly—the elephant's / sign of defeat—he resisted, but is the child // of reason now. [15] Indeed, Moore seems to have given up her poetic project of meaning more than she can express. In "Spenser's Ireland" (1941), she ascribes to a credo which is based on a curtailment and confinement of energies in "captivity" of a singular belief:

> whoever again
> and again says, 'I'll never give in', never sees
>
> that you're not free
>   until you've been made captive by
>   supreme belief [16]

However, although Moore's poetry of this period reflects sadness and resignation, she seems resolved in her rejection of the impulses of her earlier poetry, unable or unwilling to maintain a sensibility that fastidiously counters the existing meanings of her culture.

The change in Moore's poetry can be clearly seen by comparing several of Moore's overstated poems of the 1940's with her earlier work. One of the frequent strategies of the later poems is to amass definitions and examples of phenomena without regard for their social contexts or for the forms of representation which constitute them. Unlike Moore's earlier poems, in which phenomena and expressions are considered with respect to their larger implications, the idealizing languages of the later poetry obscure realities that may be incompatible or problematic. Unlike Macherey's "true author," Moore no longer interrogates social contradictions, but "resolves" them through assertions of unity and of originating and singular sources. And while these poems sometimes provide altered ways of considering or appreciating certain cultural values, they almost always enlist conventional values. At their best, the promotional poems encourage somewhat innovative points of view and include depictions of others and otherness which cannot be completely contained within Moore's overriding concern with unity. [17] However, in contrast to Moore's earlier work, they rarely enact subversive encounters with dominant cultural meanings.

It is not simply coincidental, then, that in Moore's later poems she increasingly makes references to commercial entities. Although as early as "Poetry," Moore argued for the inclusion of "'business documents and / school books,'" not until her later poetry does she readily include the anti-poetic language of such commercial trade names as "Bell Telephone Laboratories," "The John Day Company," the "pale-ale-eyed impersonal look / which the sales-placard gives the bock beer buck," and "a taslon shirt . . . sewn by Excello."[18] Since in her later poetry Moore's aesthetic is largely one of abstracting values and attributes—validating whatever can be validated and ignoring the rest—she can include the peculiar gains produced by an American economy without considering the larger implications of these. By contrast, in "People's Surroundings" (1922), Moore studies and questions the relation between the products of high culture and commercial culture:

> there is something attractive about a mind that moves in a
>   straight line—
> the municipal bat-roost of mosquito warfare, concrete
>   statuary,
> medicaments for "instant beauty" in the hands of all,
> and that live wire, the American string quartette;
> these are questions more than answers

In this earlier poem, Moore is as concerned with bringing out differences between elements as with their similarities. Further, she takes into consideration larger social contexts and processes. Thus, "the American string quartette" may be a "live wire" because it exists in an aggressive commercial culture of " 'instant beauty.' "[19]

Although in "The Mind Is an Enchanting Thing" (1943) Moore makes allusions primarily to high culture, her commodified definitions and examples of the mind's "enchanting" powers suggests her changed relation to the larger American culture.[20] In amassing her definitions and examples, Moore celebrates the mind's capacity for unity and for unified action over its capacity for differentiation and particular behaviors. Central control is simply asserted: the mind is "trued by regnant certainty." While the mind's "inconsistencies" are mentioned, they are reigned in under the controlling nomenclature of a "conscientious inconsistency" and Scarlatti's artful musical compositions. In fact, the very multiplicity of the mind's parts seems to insure its ultimate unity, as the mind is like "the glaze on a / katydid-wing / subdivided by sun / til the nettings are legion." While the poem is not without its opposing terms, these are not contrarieties or even agreeing differences, but affiliates. Thus, the "legion" of the mind can "take apart / dejection." The poem's concluding lines provide an unintentional confession. By asserting that the mind is "not a Herod's oath that cannot change," Moore draws attention to the ways in which her own singular definitions are themselves little Herod's oaths that do not change, at a great distance from her earlier poetry of ambiguity, multivalency, and unrepresentability.

Certainly, Moore's concern with unity in "The Mind Is an Enchanting Thing" is at a far remove from many of her earlier poems, especially "An Octopus," in which she criticizes the Greeks for "resolving with benevolent conclusiveness / 'complexities that will be complexities / as long as the world lasts.'" It is also in marked contrast to Moore's "To the Peacock of France," in which the powers of Molière's mind are praised. In this early, fantastic poem, Moore does not praise the mind's unity but rather Molière's writerly capabilities, demonstrating, rather than simply asserting, those powers through her own writing. Playing with the multivalencies of literal and symbolic registers, Moore convincingly unfurls the peacock's tail at the end of the poem. While Molière has charmed the rogue Scaramouche's color away, Moore herself has adversely charmed Molière's hidden color into being.

In "Four Quartz Crystal Clocks" (1940), Moore attends to a form of perfect central control—the four "workless" clocks that "tell time intervals to other clocks." In this poem Moore's very concern with accuracy as repetition reveals her increasing pull toward metaphoric and symbolic, as opposed to metonymic and literal, structures. Moore draws attention to the extreme sensitivity of the clocks, and their necessary removal to a rarified atmosphere:

> a quartz prism when
> the temperature changes, feels
>   the change and that the then
> electrified alternate edges
>   oppositely charged, threaten
>   careful timing; so that
>
> this water-clear crystal as the Greeks used to say,
>   this "clear ice" must be kept at the

> same coolness. Repetition, with
>   the scientist, should be
> synonymous with accuracy.

Moore would have us appreciate the human effort necessary to maintain this perfect functioning, suggesting that it is human control of
the environment, a constant monitoring, which allows for machine-
like accuracy. While Moore is undoing in part the cultural belief or
fear that machines may function more perfectly than humans, she is
also enlisting the hierarchical dualism between human and machine,
privileging the human. Indeed, despite Moore's fascination with
these inhuman "worksless" clocks, she seems morally impelled to
demonstrate their dependence on human activity.

In contrast, Moore's collage poem, "Bowls" (1923), is anti-human-
ist in its demonstration of how certain phenomena are not adequately represented by a meaning system in which symbolic and
metaphoric thought is privileged over literal and metonymic elements. In "Bowls," Moore de-privileges the human in order to disclose non-human attributes. In urging the "meanings" of a quickness
that either cuts through or adds layers, Moore discloses how meanings may be dependent on such non-humanly controlled phenomena
as movement, change, and quickness. For as "precisians," we are "not
citizens of Pompeii arrested in action / as a cross-section of one's
correspondence would seem to imply."

In "What Are Years?" (1940), as in other poems, such as "In Distrust of Merits" and "'Keeping Their World Large,'" which explicitly
address her concerns arising from World War II, Moore focuses her
attention away from "a direct treatment of the 'thing,'" and engages
in largely abstract and symbolic forms of thinking.[21] Concerning the
attainment of strength through adversity and resignation, "What Are
Years?" employs images of surface and depth with their respective
associations of superficiality and profundity in an entirely conventional way:

> He
> sees deep and is glad, who
>   accedes to mortality
> and in his imprisonment, rises
> upon himself as

the sea in a chasm, struggling to be
free and unable to be
in its surrendering
finds its continuing.

The contrast to "The Fish," an earlier meditation on the sea, could
not be more marked. In "The Fish," the perspective is deliberately
without depth, without a specular insight into things, for "the chasm
side is dead." Rather than invoking the limitless power of the depths
of the sea, Moore focuses on the limited power of the surface of the
edifice. Indeed, the sense of power in "The Fish" is associated with
things in themselves, not what they symbolize.

In "Silence" (1924) and "Propriety" (1944), Moore addresses the
significance of reticence and restraint. [22] But whereas in "Silence,"
Moore questions the meaning of restraint for different speakers in
different situations, "Propriety" simply proposes definitions and examples of reticent behavior, apart from any larger cognitive or con-
textual considerations. Thus, propriety is "a tuned reticence with
rigour / from strength at the source," and "it's not a graceful sadness,"
but "resistance with bent head." Whereas in her earlier poems, there
is no singular "strength at the source," but only shifting contexts and
shifting meanings, Moore now simply asserts this "source" and promotes her particular brand of propriety. Some persons and some phenomena just seem to have it:

The fish-spine
on firs, on
sombre trees
by the sea's
walls of wave-worn rock—have it; and
a moonbow and Bach's cheerful firmness
in a minor key.

In "Silence," Moore simultaneously praises and criticizes a decorum
of restraint, revealing the power relations that allow some to be restrained and condemn others to silence. Moore enacts the decorum
of restraint in this understated poem, while waging a quite bitter
attack on her exemplar of restraint, the father. While much of the
interest and subtlety of "Silence" depends on the ways silence and
restraint are contextualized and played off one another, "Propriety"

only provides fixed definitions, "Bach's cheerful firmness / in a minor key."

Although I do not aim to provide a comprehensive analysis of Moore's later poems, I will focus my concluding exposition on two groups of poems from her later work which yield further insight into the relationship between Moore's gender and her poetic production. The first group is from the 1930's, when Moore wrote several poems which as descriptions of animals are also forms of self-portraiture. In her earlier poems, animals provide the occasion for inconclusive and comprehensive forms of inquiry; in the later poems they are the basis for the formation of identity—identities which bear more than a passing relation to Moore's own projected self-image and aesthetic commitments. Indeed, such animal poems as "The Jerboa," "The Frigate Pelican," and "The Plumet Basilisk," written at a time when she was trying to re-emerge as a poet, are perhaps her most direct attempts at self-portraiture—and the poetry is among her most traditionally symbolic or specular.[23]

Throughout this book, I have suggested that Moore's work is anti-specular in its impulses. But if Moore's poetry can be seen as a refusal of specular discourse, of an egotistical sublime, or of the Lacanian imaginary within the realm of the symbolic, it is not a complete rejection of an imaginary or specular writing.[24] My argument that Moore's poetry remains vital only in so far as she attempts to write a universal poetry that includes her perspective as a woman suggests that Moore's writing is in some way an attempt to "see" or "represent" herself—to enlist the imaginary or specular possibilities of representation. Indeed, Moore's anti-specular poetry likely emerges out of an intense desire to locate herself within her culture's symbolic orders. In her earlier poetry, this desire results in an intense peering into others and estranged phrases in which she sees herself only insofar as she fails to see herself. In her later poetry, she largely gives up this quest, no longer attempting to write a poetry in which she represents both herself and her culture. Distanced from her initial quest, she writes a poetry of overstatement, which simply promotes beneficial aspects of her culture. In between these two groups of poems are several poems which combine aspects of both groups, and Moore's desire to see herself gives over to a specular or symbolic poetry.

In her initial work of the 1930's, then, Moore continues to attempt to "see" herself, to "represent" herself, in her verse, but she strays from her earlier stance ("elsewhere") in her search for the clarity and permanence of self-reflecting portraits. And while the multiplicity of animal poems and their sometimes contradictory themes suggest that Moore is unable or unwilling to establish a unified self-portrait, the individual poems comprise a far less comprehensive identity quest than do her earlier poems. Indeed, as with most of the later poems, it is far easier to discern what these poems are about than the earlier poems whose significance is frequently in the encounter depicted. Ironically, then, as Moore engages in the seemingly narcissistic luxury of forming images of herself and of her poetic concerns, she is also moving away from herself. As Irigaray, among others, has suggested, for women situated within phallogocentric languages there can be no life-enhancing forms of specularity, no self-reflecting narcissism.[25]

The second group of poems I will consider were written from the late 1930's through the 50's and promote "feminine" attributes. One of Moore's responses to a troubling world is to develop an aesthetic and morality of maternal care. But as in her other promotional poems, no longer concerned with how qualities and attributes inhere in social realities as well as in forms of representation, Moore simply affirms feminine and maternal qualities in poems such as "Bird-Witted," "The Paper Nautilus," "He 'Digesteth Harde Yron,'" "A Carriage from Sweden," and "The Arctic Ox (or Goat)."[26] In comparison to earlier poems, such as "Roses Only" and "Marriage," in which gender is specifically at issue, Moore's later poems largely reinscribe existing gender determinations, falling far short of her poetics of gynesis.[27]

In many respects, Moore's animal poems of the 1930's constitute a writing directly between her earlier poetry of encounter and understatement and her later poetry of promotion and overstatement. As efforts to establish forms of identity, these poems maintain Moore's earlier impulse to represent herself; but in their desire for fixed and stable identities, they necessarily tend toward a promotional writing. It would be a mistake, of course, to suggest that Moore's animal poems of the 1932–36 period are in any way simplistic, for their descriptions and meditations are extensive. However, these descriptions and meditations are circumscribed by the need to establish coherent forms of identity, unlike the earlier poetry. For example, the figure of the fish in "The Fish" establishes a nominal coherence that frees the poem from demands for discursive coherence. In contrast, her later animal poems exist within relatively fixed discursive and symbolic frameworks. Furthermore, in the case of the jerboa (the rat), the frigate pelican, and the plumet basilisk, Moore elects to write about animals which have a considerable relationship to herself. All of the Moore family members took on animal nicknames, inspired in part by the *Wind in the Willows*; and rat and basilisk were important names for Moore throughout much of her life.[28] In addition, the habits of the scavenging frigate pelican resemble Moore's poetic practice of scavenging verbal expressions.

By first considering the early animal portrait, "Black Earth" (1918), the relatively fixed and stable qualities of animals in the later poems are made apparent. In "Black Earth," Moore suggests that the very concept of identity is problematical; at times, the "I" of the poem declares itself to be the elephant to which "black earth" refers, yet it also undercuts this identification. The poem begins with an unidentified "I" who compares its behavior to that of the "hippopotamus" or "alligator," and contrarily declares, "I do these / things which I do, which please / no one but myself." Furthermore, the "I" states that she only "inhabits" "this elephant skin," but then attests to its impenetrability, inviolability, and thickness. By the speaker's proclaiming herself to be a "renaissance" peculiarly identified by its "blemishes that stand up and shout," Moore calls attention to the contradiction inherent in the identification of such large, phenomenal animals as the elephant, alligator, and hippopotamus by their small and peculiar bumps. Furthermore, while the sediment of the river which encrusts these animals joints is mere "patina of circumstance," if done away with, "I am myself done away with."

Indeed, "Black Earth" suggests that identity and the means by which it is achieved may involve dichotomies and dichotomous images. The poem posits, on the one hand, the human—"that tree trunk without / roots"—with its arbitrary identity—"The I of each is to / the I of each, / a kind of fretful speech / which sets a limit on itself"; and, on the other hand, the elephant, whose "soul shall never / be cut into / by a wooden spear" and whose "name means thick." And while the poem inquires into two sources of identity, external poise and spiritual poise, it conceives of identity as maintained from

151

without "by . . . what strange pressure of the atmosphere" as well as from within as a "substance / needful as an instance / of the indestructibility of matter." Furthermore, positing an indivisible entity whose "soul shall never / be cut into / by a wooden spear," the poem also raises the possibility that the qualities of depth and thickness are largely perceptual, accessible only to those who can see through them:

> Will
> depth be depth, thick skin be thick, to one who can
>   see no
> beautiful element of unreason under it.

The poem may well be an "adverse" reaction to the simple dichotomies of Eliot's poem, "The Hippopotamus," published several months before Moore's poem. In "The Hippopotamus," Eliot satirizes the hypocrisy of a spiritual and intellectual church by showing the relative goodness of an unthinking and fleshly hippopotamus. While Eliot's exposé on an animal may have appealed to Moore, his dichotomies may have been far too reductive for her, for although Moore establishes a dichotomy between elephant and human, she also undermines it. And, unlike Eliot, she is bemused by the human: "that tree trunk without / roots, accustomed to shout / its own thoughts to itself like shell." On closer inspection, elephants and humans share more in common in Moore's poem than might initially seem to be the case, for while the human is represented as a "wand" and a "tree trunk without / roots," the elephant is identified as "black earth preceded by a tendril." Indeed, while the elephant sees and hears, the human is made "to see and not see; to hear and not hear." Human nature, thus, is not reducible to the merely physical, and if this "not seeing" and "not hearing" allow for hypocrisy, they also open up the possibility for a "spiritual poise." In "Black Earth," Moore would seem to wish to encounter the mysteries of man and beast, which, after all, cannot be so simply dichotomized, as both possess "the beautiful element of unreason." The poem questions, but does not resolve, the nature of power and of spirit, suggesting that to fix these entities, even as Eliot satirically does in his poem, is to fail to perceive or know them.

In contrast to the ambiguity of "Black Earth," "The Jerboa" and

"The Frigate Pelican" employ animals that are symbolic or exemplary of characteristics and attributes sought by Moore in her person and in her artistic works. Both animals are praised for their quickness, self-protectiveness, elusiveness, restlessness, removal, subtlety, and inner-direction. Charles Molesworth has suggested that the two parts of "The Jerboa"—"Too Much" and "Abundance"—concern Moore's move at this time away from her cosmopolitan life in Manhattan as editor of *The Dial,* to Brooklyn, and her retired, "'diffident'" life there.[29] Indeed, Moore, who may have been at least partially ambivalent about this move, relinquishing her intense life in Manhattan for a desired seclusion in Brooklyn, admires both the rat and the pelican for their ability to engage in activity and then to rest.

But if "The Jerboa" and "The Frigate Pelican" share important characteristics, they are also opposites. The jerboa's genius is his capacity for his close and imitative relationship to his environment, whereas the pelican's genius is for a distant and circumspect vision of those far beneath him. The jerboa achieves his ends in part through his ability to flatten himself against the earth; conversely, the frigate pelican attains his objectives because of the heights to which he can ascend. While both camouflage with their surroundings—the rat by assuming the color of sand, and the pelican by "keeping at a height / so great the feathers look black and the beak does not / show"—their different vantage points entail divergent views about their activities or their "art," and their relation to others. While the jerboa may well symbolize the non-hierarchizing and fluid perspective of Moore's early poetry, the frigate pelican represents a newer desire to see from on high and to fix visions at a distance. The fact that Moore explores each of these possibilities separately—developing them as separate identities—suggests that in this poetry she has given up her earlier attempt to be comprehensive. Indeed, in Moore's earlier poems, perspective itself is problematized, and horizontal and vertical as well as close and distant perspectives are confounded.

Of "The Jerboa" (1932) and "The Frigate Pelican" (1934), the first is in many ways the more complex poem. Divided into two sections, "The Jerboa" portrays "Too Much," a civilization which is characterized by its hierarchical social order and the possessiveness of its inhabitants, and "Abundance," characterized by the independent jerboa who has "nothing but plenty." Although the society of "Too Much" is not without its appeal and redeeming features, it is clearly the lesser of the two possibilities. Even though Moore seems to admire the inventiveness of the civilization of "Too Much," she criticizes its wastefulness, a wastefulness not only caused by the over-consumption among its privileged classes, but also by an imprecise and mechanical use of resources due to the imperiousness of the chain of command. Thus, "Too Much" "is a picture" of a civilization whose inventions are made possible, as well as characterized, by a prevailing "fine distance." Indeed, the society's forms of mimicry and reflection are exercises in the mere copying of appearances:

> Lords and ladies put goose-grease
> paint in round bone boxes with pivoting
> lid incised with the duck-wing
>
> or reverted duck-
> head; kept in a buck
> or rhinoceros horn,
> the ground horn; and locust oil in stone locusts.

The king both gives his name and is named for the serpents and beetles of his kingdom, which are replicated as statues and portraits. And, in a society made up of those who "everywhere" have "Power over the poor," "dwarfs" lend "a fantasy and a verisimilitude" to the representation, whimsically representing the suppressed class.

In contrast, the jerboa's mimicry is so precise that he "honors the sand by assuming its colour / closed upper-paws seeming one with the fur in its flight from danger." Accordingly, an art which would attain to the excellent standards exemplified by the jerboa would mimic an object's essence or principles, rather than its superficial appearance. Moore concludes her poem by stilling the jerboa into art:

> Its leaps should be set
> to the flageolet;
>   pillar body erect
>   on a three-cornered smooth-working Chippendale
>   claw—propped on hind legs, and tail as third toe,
>   between leaps to its burrow.

Certainly the concluding image of the fast-moving rat and the Chippendale chair is a testament to Moore's artistic capabilities. The comparison between the jerboa's "pillar body intact" and the "three-cornered smooth-working Chippendale / claw" is masterful. However, the juxtaposition suggests a counter-testimony to itself, similar to the reference to a "Herod's oath" in "Propriety." That this "free-born" and "untouched" rat should finally inspire a "Chippendale claw"—life becoming furniture—is troublesome.

Many of Moore's 1930's poems address the process of a simple reflection and mimesis, which is frequently associated with a kind of deadness and loss of power or force. In "Virginia Britannica," there is "the lead- / gray lead legged mocking-bird with head / held halfway, and / meditative eye as dead / as sculptured marble."[30] The Psyche figure of "Half-Deity," whose "talk was as strange as my grandmother's muff," has "Mirror eyes / of strong anxiety."[31] One of the pigeons in Moore's uncollected poem, "Pigeons," is a "Mocker with one eye / destroyed." The poem concludes with a "new pigeon humbly dedicated to / the Gentlemen of the / Feather Club."[32] In turning to a symbolic or specular poetry in the 1930's, Moore's poetry is haunted by the deadness of the impulse toward mimesis for a woman writer of her "conscious" and "unconscious fastidiousness."

Although in "The Jerboa" Moore criticizes a hierarchical society, in "The Frigate Pelican" the titular bird is admired quite simply for his power over others and for his view from on high. Calling the pelican "dishonest" at one point in the poem, Moore, in her feature exposé, also presents his scavenging and stealing in a favorable light. Rather than fish for himself, "he appears to prefer // to take, on the wing, from industrious cruder-winged species / the fish they have caught," and is a "marvel of grace." Furthermore, Moore does not seem concerned that his view from on high makes the activities of those below appear pathetic: "ants / keeping house all their lives in the crack of a / crag with no view from the top." In her tribute to this bird Moore composes many remarkable images, but the perspective of the poem is not very comprehensive. And the singularity of the poem's perspective, duplicated by the singularity of the frigate pelican's vantage point, suggests how far Moore had come from her earlier poetry, written from "elsewhere" about "An Octopus" with "no weather side."

Although the publication date of "The Plumet Basilisk" (1933) locates it between "The Jerboa" (1932) and "The Frigate Pelican" (1934), Moore probably initiated work on it long before either of

the other poems, as parts of it appear in her poetry notebook from
1923.[33] And, if there is one transitional poem between her earlier,
understated poetry and her later, overstated work, it is "The Plumet
Basilisk." In this poem Moore's earlier commitment to elusive, fluid,
and unrepresentable meanings are in tension with, as well as symbolized by, her depiction of camouflaging lizards. The poem's dual
impulse toward and away from fixity and symbolization is clearly
revealed in a statement about the plumet basilisk toward the conclusion of the poem:

> No anonymous
> nightingale sings in a swamp, fed on
> sound . . .
> This is our Tower-of-London
> jewel that the Spaniards failed to see

Although Moore is, on the one hand, attempting to locate a very
particular symbol for a New World poetry and probably for her own
poetry, an important aspect of the symbol is that it is not always
visible.

"The Plumet Basilisk," among Moore's finest works, is compelling
in its overdetermined conflicts. Throughout the poem, Moore portrays moments of appearance and disappearance. The poem begins
with the appearance of the basilisk and concludes with its disappearance, remarking, in both instances, on its intermittence:

> In blazing driftwood
> the green keeps showing at the same place;
> as, intermittently, the fire-opal shows blue and green.
> In Costa Rica the true Chinese lizard face
> is found, of the amphibious falling dragon, the living firework.

> he is alive there
> in his basilisk cocoon beneath
> the one of living green; his quicksilver ferocity
> quenched in the rustle of his fall into the sheath
> which is the shattering sudden splash that marks his
> temporary loss.

Unlike Moore's earlier poems, in which forms of contrariety and agreeing difference allow for the expression of contradictions Moore encounters in representing herself and her concerns, in "The Plumet Basilisk" she seeks a metaphoric or symbolic meaning—a "green that keeps showing at the same place"—without completely relinquishing her earlier sense of meaning as unrepresentable. As the poem quips, "the plumet portrays / mythology's wish / to be interchangeably man and fish"—that is, to be solidly human and elusively nonhuman. However, as in other animal poems of this period, Moore's search for positive forms of representation necessitates filling in the gaps (or refusals) of her earlier poetry. Thus, unlike "Sea Unicorns and Land Unicorns," which explores the textures of different forms of representation, "The Plumet Basilisk" opts for a writing which is comparatively seamless and which develops a consistent perspective about multiple phenomena. As Bonnie Costello notes: "Finding herself divided in a world of multiple perspectives and interests, Moore projects the struggle onto a unified figure whose existence depends upon fending off finite definitions." The figure of the basilisk as represented in mythology "is not only the creature whose look can kill, but also that creature who expires when someone holds up a mirror and forces him to confront his own image."[34]

In fact, several camouflaging lizards along with the plumet basilisk are represented in this poem—the Malay dragon, the Tuatera, the frilled lizard, the three-horned chameleon, and sea lizards—with their popular and scientific names and additional information about them supplied in Moore's notes. And while Moore's impulse in the poem is to represent forms of unity, it is a unity bristling and all but shattered by multiplicity and diversity. The section entitled "The Tuatera" begins:

> Elsewhere, sea lizards—
>   congregated so there is not room
> to step, with tails laid criss-cross, alligator-style among
>   birds toddling in and out—are innocent of whom
> they neighbor. Bird-reptile social life is pleasing. The
>   tuatera
>
> will tolerate a
>   petrel in its den, and lays ten eggs

Furthermore, Moore's earlier commitment to unrepresentable meanings—her refusal to make coherent meanings but rather to display
"contrarieties" and "agreeing differences"—may well be remaindered
in this poem in her remarkable references to darkness and hollow
music. She compares the basilisk's tail to "piano keys" that

> are barred
> by five black stripes across the white. This octave of faulty
>   decorum hides the extraordinary lizard
> till night-fall, which is for man the basilisk whose look will
>   kill; but is

> for lizards men can
>   kill, the welcome dark—with the galloped
> ground-bass of the military drum, the squeak of bag-pipes
>   and of bats. Hollow whistled monkey-notes disrupt
> the castanets. Taps from the back of the bow sound odd on
>   last year's gourd

Indeed, Moore's portrayal of sound as both piercing and hollow en-
hances the poem's preoccupation with alternating presences and ab-
sences.

As in "Sea Unicorns and Land Unicorns," Moore's concern with
the relationship between reflection and identity uncannily replicates
the mirror stage of the Lacanian imaginary. The plumet basilisk seeks
to establish a moment of absolute identity with itself—only to destroy the idealizing mirror by diving into Guatavita Lake with its
hidden goddess:

> He leaps and meets his
>   likeness in the stream and, king with king,
> helped by his three-part plume along the back, runs on two
>   legs,
>   tail dragging; faints upon the air; then with a spring
> dives to the stream-bed, hiding as the chieftain with gold
>   body hid in

> Guatavita Lake.

The goddess of Guatavita Lake is doubly hidden, once in the lake
and again in Moore's notes: "The king, painted with gums and pow-

dered with gold-dust as symbolic of the sun, the supreme deity, was each year escorted by his nobles on a raft, to the centre of the lake, in a ceremonial of tribute to the goddess of the lake." As with the unicorn hiding its head in the lap of the lady—its reciprocating reflection—specularity is momentarily done away with. In the conclusion of the poem, a highly overdetermined moment of the loss of reflection and specularity, is represented. As the basilisk disappears, he is already hidden in his cocoon. Furthermore, a synesthesia of sound, visual and kinetic elements intensifies his disappearance: "His quicksilver ferocity / quenched in the rustle of his fall into the sheath / which is the shattering sudden splash that marks his temporary loss."

It is tempting to finish my account of Moore's poetry with the achievement of "The Plumet Basilisk." However, in order to conclude the analysis of the relationship between Moore's gender and her poetic production, I will show how Moore's later poetry abandons her earlier investigation into how gender inheres in forms of representation, and simply promotes specific feminine qualities. In comparison to such earlier poems as "Those Various Scalpels," "Roses Only," and "Marriage," in which Moore focuses on the construction of gender, in "Bird-Witted," "The Paper Nautilus," "He 'Digesteth Harde Yron,'" "A Carriage From Sweden," and "The Arctic Ox (or Goat)," she merely affirms feminine and maternal characteristics. Indeed, during the last twenty years of her career, Moore seems far less interested in considering differences among gendered positions than in valorizing acts of care.

Although "Bird-Witted," "The Paper Nautilus," and "He 'Digesteth Harde Yron'" all espouse moralities of maternal care, their formal differences reveal Moore's willingness to abstract values from larger cultural and representational orders. As in her other promotional poems, these poems are structured around oppositions in which one side is upheld over the other. And while it is still a notable feature of Moore's poetry that she partially maintains through intricate descriptions the otherness of others, the poems are circumscribed by their impulses to symbolize and to exemplify.

In "Bird-Witted," one of Moore's few narrative poems, she compares unfavorably the "intellectual cautious- / ly creeping cat" who clumsily seeks out his own desserts with the instinctive, quick,

accurate movements of the mother bird, motivated by the safety of
her children:

> Towards the high-keyed intermittent squeak
>   of broken carriage-springs, made by
> the three similar, meek-
>   coated bird's eye
> freckled forms she comes; and when
> from the beak
>   of one, the still living
>   beetle has dropped
> out, she picks it up and puts
> it in again. . . .
>   What delightful note
>   with rapid unexpected flute-
> sounds leaping from the throat
>   of the astute
> grown bird, comes back to one from
> the remote
>   unenergetic sun-
>   lit air before
> the brood was here? Why has the
> bird's voice become
>   harsh? A piebald cat observing them,
>   is slowly creeping toward the trim
> trio on the tree-stem.
>   Unused to him
> the three make room—uneasy
> new problem.
>   A dangling foot that missed
>   its grasp, is raised
> and finds the twig on which it
> planned to perch. The
>   parent darting down, nerved by what chills
>   the blood, and by hope rewarded—
> of toil—since nothing fills
>   squeaking unfed
> mouths, wages deadly combat,
>   and half kills

> with bayonet beak and
> cruel wings, the
> intellectual cautious-
> l y   c r e e p i n g   c a t.

Although most of "Bird-Witted" is told from the vantage of the birds'
nest, Moore briefly breaks the ongoing present of her narrative to
include a vision of "the remote / unenergetic sun- / lit air before / the
brood was here." Like the presence of the piebald cat, the thought of
the brood's previous and utter absence creates a pall. The small aside
gives a dusky center to the poem, as powerful as the unspeakable
truths of sexuality and kinship central to many of Faulkner's fiction.

If "Bird-Witted" depends for its meaning on a conventional narrative sequence and the contrast between the quick instinctive bird and
the slow, intellectual cat, "The Paper Nautilus" is unified through its
central symbol, a chambered nautilus shell, and an opposition between inner and outer. The poem, in fact, was written as a gift to
Elizabeth Bishop in return for her gift to Moore of an actual nautilus
shell. Moore herself seems to have had mothering as well as mentor-
ing inclinations toward the younger Bishop—a kind of mothering
that, like the nurturance provided by the chambered nautilus and
Moore's own mother, helps by hindering the young. Indeed, as noted
previously, Moore seemed to have taken on the behavior of her own
mother and urged Bishop—contrary to Bishop's own poetic interests—to express "significant values."

"The Paper Nautilus," about the act of creation as maternal protec-
tiveness and watchfulness, moves from images of an externality, to an
internality, and back again:

> For authorities whose hopes
> are shaped by mercenaries?
>   Writers entrapped by
>   teatime fame and by
> commuters' comforts? Not for these
>   the paper nautilus
>   constructs her thin glass shell.
>
>   Giving her perishable
> souvenir of hope, a dull
>   white outside and smooth-

edged inner surface
glossy as the sea, the watchful
   maker of it guards it
   day and night; she scarcely

   eats until the eggs are hatched.
Buried eight-fold in her eight
   arms, for she is in
   a sense a devil-
fish, her glass ramshorn-cradled freight
   is hid but is not crushed.
   As Hercules, bitten

by a crab loyal to the hydra,
was hindered to succeed,
   the intensively
   watched eggs coming from
the shell free it when they are freed, —
   leaving its wasp-nest flaws
   of white on white, and close-

laid Ionic chiton-folds
like the lines in the mane of
   a Parthenon horse,
   round which the arms had
wound themselves as if they knew love
   is the only fortress
   strong enough to trust to.

The poem initially repudiates external enclosures—"teatime fame" and "commuters' comforts"—in the interest of its own definition of an internal and internalized enclosure, love, outwardly symbolized by the nautilus shell. The internality which the poem proposes, while highly intimate, is not stifling: the paper nautilus may "bury" the eggs but it does not "crush" them. The strength of the eggs to free themselves is emphasized by comparing them to Hercules who, although "bitten by a crab loyal to the hydra," succeeded in killing the hydra. The paper nautilus, as both crab and hydra, keeps her young eggs from hatching too easily, lest in reaching their full size too quickly they are *hindered* to succeed, rather than hindered to *succeed.* (The ambiguity of "hindered to succeed" may be an insider's joke for Bishop, an acknowledgment by Moore of the potentially negative effects of an intense maternal watchfulness.) The poem concludes with its own freed eggs—an external image of arms wound around a Parthenon horse, freely electing love—that links an internal love to its outer appearance, its "chiton-folds."

Despite its appealing and careful definitions, "The Paper Nautilus," in comparison with Moore's earlier poems, depends on and reinscribes the conventional oppositions of internal and external, valuing the former over the latter. In "He 'Digesteth Harde Yron,'" Moore assumes a similar dichotomy, stating that "the power of the visible / is the invisible" and noting that certain kinds of meanings are "always missed / by the externalist." Moving away from her symbolic impulses in "The Paper Nautilus," Moore in this later poem creates a small tableau emblematic of a "bald" moral. That is, the poem upholds the ostrich, characterized by his "maternal concentration," intelligent suspiciousness, integrity, and justice, over the unheroic, greedy obviousness of persons who would exploit the resources of this "sparrow-camel" in an ugly and static display of wealth. Again, although Moore's illustration is subordinate to her message, the wonderful intricacy and strangeness of her depiction maintain some of the qualities of the earlier poetry:

> This bird watches his chicks with
> a maternal concentration, after
>   he has sat on the eggs
>   at night six weeks, his legs
> their only weapon of defence.
> He is swifter than a horse;
>   he has a foot hard
>   as a hoof; the leopard
> is not more suspicious.

> Six hundred ostrich-brains served
> at one banquet, the ostrich-plume-tipped tent
>   and desert spear, jewel-
>   gorgeous ugly egg-shell
> goblets, eight pairs of ostriches

> in harness, dramatize a
> meaning always missed
> by the externalist.

Given the larger culture, Moore's promotion of feminine or maternal care as a primary cultural value may be seen as fairly radical, yet she no longer seems to want to examine all that is entailed in being constructed as a woman as well as a feminine care-giver. Indeed, as early as "The Frigate Pelican," she promotes a vision which would disregard, rather than deconstruct, differences between men and women as they are culturally engendered and representationally inscribed. Thus the pelican who, "as impassioned Handel," "never was known to have fallen in love," does "not know Gretel from Hansel." In contrast, in her somewhat earlier, and more ambitious poem, "The Jerboa," she plays with gendered differences:

> Princes
> clad in queens' dresses
> calla or petunia
>   white that trembled at the edge, and queens in a
>   king's underskirt of fine-twilled thread like silk-
>   worm gut, as bee-man and milk-
>
> maid, kept divine cows
> and bees.

Indeed, Moore's earlier decentered, understated, and more playful poetry may have seemed insufficient to her in the face of a number of personal and public crises, and, like many feminists, she may have seen the increasing value of promoting the virtues of maternal care. However, whereas early in 1930, Moore wrote to her brother that she didn't want to sacrifice either her vision or fame, by the 1940's she proclaimed that poetry in time of war doesn't need technical virtuosity.[35] But, as has been shown, if Moore lessened her "technical virtuosity" in these later poems, she also diminished her vision.

AFTERWORD

Thus, the silence . . . is not a lack to be remedied, or an inadequacy to be made up for. It is not a temporary silence that could be finally abolished. We must distinguish the necessity of this silence. For example, it can be shown that it is the juxtaposition and conflict of several meanings which produce the radical otherness which shapes the work: this conflict is not resolved or absorbed, but simply *displayed*. . . . In its every particle the work *manifests*, uncovers, what it cannot say. This silence gives it life.

—Pierre Macherey, *A Theory of Literary Production*[1]

Must this multiplicity of female desire and female language be understood as shards, scattered remnants of a violated sexuality? A sexuality denied? The question has no simple answer. The rejection, the exclusion of a female imaginary, puts woman in the position of experiencing herself only fragmentarily, in the little-structured margins of a dominant ideology, as waste, or excess, what is left of a mirror invested by the (masculine) "subject" to reflect himself, to copy himself. Moreover, the role of "femininity" is prescribed by this masculine specula(riza)tion and corresponds scarcely at all to women's desire, which may be recovered only in secret, in hiding, with anxiety and guilt.

—Luce Irigiray, *This Sex Which Is Not One*[2]

Throughout this study, I have suggested that Moore's poetry of understatement written before 1935 is significant precisely because of the refusals, or silences, which shape it. Indeed, the lasting fascination of Moore's verse for her readers is most likely

165

related to the "life" created by her "conscious" and "unconscious fastidious" refusals of language and representational conventions which underwrite existing gender determinations.

In their insightful essays on Moore, Hugh Kenner and Helen Vendler provide provocative, but seemingly contradictory, descriptions of Moore and her earlier poetry. Kenner remarks, "at her best, she was other from us, and her subjects other from her."[3] In seeming opposition, Vendler remarks that Moore's earlier poetry "represents one of the most individual, private, and conclusive inquiries into identity ever brought into print by an American woman."[4] While these statements might initially appear to be at odds, they can be seen as complementary, providing Moore's problematical relationship to the literary tradition and representational conventions is brought under scrutiny. Indeed, Moore's earlier poetry is "one of the most . . . conclusive inquiries into identity ever brought into print by an American woman," if that quest is understood as one that explores others and expressions which are not self-reflections, but "other from her."

Moore, of course, was not the only woman of her generation who struggled directly with problems of meaning and expression. Certainly H. D. and Gertrude Stein shared Moore's frustration that they could not always mean what they expressed or express what they meant. All three women in different ways encounter the limitations of a language of "masculine specula(riza)tion." In H. D., this dilemma with language leads her to posit a reality outside of language. Rachel Du Plessis comments that this "stance beyond language" is directly related to H. D.'s representation of a "feminine/maternal psyche . . . at the core of 'real' reality, a substratum beneath interpretation, only capable of being hidden or revealed."[5] However, while in such important works as *Trilogy*, H. D. extends the definition and sense of power of a feminine/maternal psyche, she also replicates masculine portrayals of the feminine.[6]

Gertrude Stein engages the problem of meaning and expression by attempting to modify syntactical and semantic sense. Although she describes her writing as "a disembodied way of disconnecting something from anything and anything from something," Stein also finds that in her attempt to do away with "sense," she can't put words together without making sense: "I took individual words and thought about them until I got their weight and volume complete and put them next to one another and at this same time I found very soon that there is no such thing as putting them together without sense."[7] Stein in her deconstruction and reconstruction of language largely avoids H. D.'s problem of reinscribing feminine stereotypes, but she does so in a language sometimes severely, if provocatively, cut off from existing forms of cultural representation. For if Stein discloses and reconstitutes the material basis of language, her writing is also frequently disembodied from existing, recognizable forms of representation.

Moore's poetry of understatement is structured by her paradoxical attempt to give expression to a universality and also to herself as a woman. While in this earlier poetry Moore works against the symbolic or specular propensities of lyric poetry, she remains compelled by the possibility of self-representation through recognizable forms of cultural representation. As such, Moore produces a poetry that marks with precision and imagination her position "elsewhere" from the estranged others and quoted expressions of her writing. But although Moore produces a set of highly significant poems, she finds them inadequate to her needs for a more definitive form of communication, turning in her later poetry to overstatement.

Both H. D.'s and Stein's writings have been more enthusiastically embraced by feminist criticism than has Moore's. Indeed, the reification of feminine presences in H. D.'s poetry and of language structures in Stein's writing make their work significant disruptions of existing forms of signification. The subversiveness of Moore's poetry is far more elusive. Rather than attempting to effect a totalizing vision or to remake language, Moore's writing offers a rich ambiguity—an ambiguity which constitutes through its elected and non-elected silences the play of her "radical otherness." In her refusal to perform surgery on a singular aspect of the literary tradition and system of representation, Moore produces a poetry which finally does not avoid, nor repeat, gender, but re-presents it.

NOTES

INTRODUCTION

1. Harold Bloom, ed., *Modern Critical Views: Marianne Moore* (New York: Chelsea House, 1987), 2.

2. Luce Irigaray, *This Sex Which Is Not One*, trans. Catherine Porter with Carolyn Burke (New York: Cornell University Press, 1985), 108.

3. Donald Hall, "The Art of Poetry: Marianne Moore. An Interview," in *Marianne Moore: A Collection of Critical Essays*, ed. Charles Tomlinson (Englewood Cliffs, New Jersey: Prentice-Hall, 1969), 27. Irigarary uses the term, "self-affection," in many instances throughout *This Sex Which Is Not One*. See especially 132–133.

4. Marianne Moore, *The Complete Prose of Marianne Moore*, ed. Patricia C. Willis (New York: Viking, 1987), 82. Moore, "When I Buy Pictures," *Observations* (New York: The Dial Press, 1924), 59. All poems written up to and including 1924, unless otherwise noted, are taken from *Observations*. Because of Moore's practice of frequent and radical revision, many versions of a poem may exist. Throughout my discussion, I use the version of a poem as it first appeared in a published volume of her verse, with the exception of those poems appearing in her first volume, *Poems* (London: The Egoist Press, 1921), which was not edited by Moore, but by her friends H. D. and Bryher.

5. Hugh Kenner, "Disliking It," in *A Homemade World* (New York: William Morrow and Company, Inc, 1975), 101.

6. Moore, "Novices," *Observations*, 72.

7. Moore, *Complete Prose*, 327–328.

8. David Kalstone, *Becoming a Poet: Elizabeth Bishop With Marianne Moore and Robert Lowell* (New York: Farrar Strauss Giroux, 1989), 90. Kalstone is quoting Moore from Elizabeth Bishop's *Collected Prose*, ed. Robert Giroux (New York: Farrar, Straus, and Giroux, 1984), 146–147.

9. F. S. Flint and Ezra Pound, "Imagisme" and "A Few Don'ts by an Imagiste," *Poetry* 1 (October 1912): 198–206.

10. In reviewing Pound's "How to Read," Moore compliments Pound for his "dual method" of "emphasis by over- and by under-statement" (*Complete Prose*, 219). One of Moore's early, unpublished critical pieces is entitled "Understatement." See The

Marianne Moore Collection, Rosenbach Museum and Library, Philadelphia, (II: 07: 03). Hereinafter this collection will be referred to as Rosenbach.

11. Moore, "In the Public Garden," in *O to Be a Dragon* (New York: Viking, 1967), 20–21.

12. In a conversation with Grace Schulman, Moore reported that she first started writing in response to "adverse ideas." See Schulman, *Marianne Moore: The Poetry of Engagement* (Chicago: University of Illinois Press, 1986), 44. "Agreeing difference" appears in Moore's poem, "Sea Unicorns and Land Unicorns," *Selected Poems* (New York: Macmillan, 1935), 105. In *Observations* (1924), the phrase is "agreeing indifference," (92). Because of the theoretical usefulness of "agreeing difference," I have decided to use this slightly later version, rather than the one in *Observations*.

13. The word "contrariety" is Moore's own invention and first appears, to my knowledge, at the bottom of a manuscript of her early poem "A Fool, A Foul Thing, A Distressful Lunatic," also titled "Masks," Rosenbach, (I: 02: 06).

14. These definitions of the "fantastic" are taken respectively from Tzvetan Todorov, *The Fantastic*, trans. Richard Howard (Ithaca, New York: Cornell University Press, 1975), and Christine Brooke-Rose, *A Rhetoric of the Unreal* (London: Cambridge University Press, 1981). Brooke-Rose considers four separate levels: literal, allegorical, moral and anagogical (68–71). I have subsumed "moral" under "allegorical" as these levels in Moore's poetry are usually merged, rather than in tension. I've also substituted the more familiar term of symbolic for anagogical.

15. Moore, "An Octopus," *Observations*, 83, 90.

16. Although several prominent critics of Moore maintain that Moore's later work is of lesser importance than her earlier work, most criticism tends to treat Moore's poetry as a consistent and unified body of work. For those critics who find Moore's later poetry disappointing in comparison to her earlier poetry, see Hugh Kenner, "Disliking It"; Robert Duncan, "Ideas of the Meaning of Form," in *Fictive Certainties* (New York: New Directions, 1955), 89–105; and John Slatin, *The Savage's Romance: The Poetry of Marianne Moore* (University Park: The Pennsylvania State University Press, 1986).

Only a few studies attempt to provide a comprehensive explanation for the chronological development of Moore's verse. Laurence Stapleton emphasizes the continuity of Moore's writing: "The contrast in form of the earlier and later poems shows an increasing ability to liberate feeling by the searching discipline of language and rhythm. . . . The poems . . . were the proofs, Marianne Moore had to find for things she had known for years. As time went on, the proofs became more comprehensible" (*Marianne Moore: The Poet's Advance* [Princeton: Princeton University Press, 1978], 156–157). Although Stapleton claims that the earlier versions of many of Moore's poems are superior to their later, revised versions, and that after "Marriage" (1923) and "An Octopus" (1924) Moore's poems do not attain the same complexity, she maintains an unflinching faith in Moore's growth as a poet. Both Schulman and Margaret Holley stress Moore's growth as a poet, given her mind's increasing capacity to fully contemplate an "objective" world (Holley, *The Poetry of Marianne Moore: A Study in Voice and Value* [Cambridge: Cambridge University Press, 1987]).

Focusing on Moore's changing attitudes to her literary predecessors and contemporaries, Slatin postulates that Moore's initial poetry is an attempt to maintain "an imperviousness" that in the end is "overwhelmed" by experience and by her awareness of her indebtedness to literary precursors. Moore's initial poetics of "resistance" is replaced by a poetics of "accommodation." Curiously, while Slatin is far more enthusiastic about Moore's earlier poetry than her later poetry, he finds Moore's earlier work shaped almost entirely by an arrogant and deceived willfulness (*The Savage's Romance*).

17. Ann Douglas, *The Feminization of American Culture* (New York: Alfred A. Knopf, 1977). Alan Trachtenberg, *The Incorporation of America: Culture and Society in Gilded Age* (New York: Hill and Wang, 1982).

18. Trachtenberg, 147.

19. Douglas, 46.

20. Charles Molesworth, *Marianne Moore, A Literary Life* (New York: Atheneum, 1990), 226.

21. Moore, "Understatement," Rosenbach, (II:07:03). Moore, "In This Age of Hard Trying Nonchalance Is Good And," *Observations*, 28.

22. Moore, *Complete Prose*, 29.

23. Molesworth, 266.

24. Irigarary, *This Sex Which Is Not One*, uses the concept "elsewhere" in many instances in her text. See, for example, 76–77.

CHAPTER 1

1. Irigaray, 80.

2. Marianne Moore to family, 28 February 1908, Rosenbach, (VI:14:03).

3. See Introduction, n. 1.

4. Ezra Pound, *The Letters of Ezra Pound*, ed. D. D. Paige (New York: Harcourt, Brace and Company, 1950), 157.

5. T. S. Eliot, "Marianne Moore (1923)," in *Marianne Moore: A Collection of Critical Essays*, ed. Charles Tomlinson (Englewood Cliffs, New Jersey: Prentice-Hall, 1969), 51.

6. Taffy Martin notes that the New Criticism instituted as fact the image Moore projected as a "decorative oddity" ("Portrait of a Writing Master: Beyond the Myth of Marianne Moore," *Twentieth Century Literature* 30, nos. 2–3 [Summer-Fall 1984]: 192).

7. R. P. Blackmur, "The Method of Marianne Moore," in *Marianne Moore: A Collection of Critical Essays*, ed. Charles Tomlinson (Englewood Cliffs, New Jersey: Prentice-Hall, 1969), 84, 85.

8. Randall Jarrell, "Her Shield," in *Marianne Moore: A Collection of Critical Essays*, ed. Charles Tomlinson (Englewood Cliffs, New Jersey: Prentice Hall, 1969), 122. In a study of Elizabeth Bishop's and Moore's relationship, David Kalstone echoes Blackmur and Jarrell: Moore's "fog and foxgloves are trained on strings"; her form and style work "to neutralize the unfathomable energy of the deep" (*Becoming a Poet* [New York: Farrar, Straus and Giroux, 1989], 54, 82). In comparisons with Bishop, Moore usually comes off poorly. Even Bonnie Costello remarks: "The world Moore entertains *is* safe despite its fallibility; Bishop's world is less comfortably balanced, less

decorative and less pastoral" ("Marianne Moore and Elizabeth Bishop: Friendship and Influence," *Twentieth Century Literature* 30, nos. 2–3 [Summer-Fall 1984], 145).

9. In 1986 when I began my study of Moore's poetry, only a few feminist studies, or even statements, about Moore's work were in existence. Since that time, several chapters and articles, but no full-length study, focusing on the relationship of Moore's gender to her poetic production have appeared. Taffy Martin (*Marianne Moore*) makes references to Moore's gender, but declines to address in any definitive way the concerns and issues of femininst criticism or theory. Other recent Moore criticism counteracts the stereotype of Moore as sexless and powerless, although none foreground the ways that Moore as a woman can "mean," can "make meaning," as I do in this study. For valuable accounts of the relationship of Moore's gender to her poetic production, see Bonnie Tymorski August, *Womanhood in Five American Poets*; Bonnie Costello, "The 'Feminine' Language of Marianne Moore"; Rachel Blau Du-Plessis, "No More of the Same: The Feminist Poetics of Marianne Moore;" Sandra Gilbert, "Marianne Moore as Female Female Impersonator"; Jeredith Merrin, *An Enabling Humility: Marianne Moore, Elizabeth Bishop, and the Uses of Tradition*; Alicia Ostriker, "Marianne Moore, the Maternal Hero, and American Women's Poetry"; Sabine Sielke, "Snapshots of Marriage, Snares of Mimicry, Snarls of Motherhood: Marianne Moore and Adrienne Rich"; and John Slatin, "Something Inescapably Typical: Questions about Gender in the Late Work of Williams and Moore." For a highly insightful account of Moore's critical relationship to her male Modernist peers as represented in her prose, see Celeste Goodridge, *Hints and Disguises: Marianne Moore and Her Contemporaries*.

10. Adrienne Rich, "When We Dead Awaken: Writing as Re-Vision," *On Lies, Secrets, and Silence: Selected Prose 1966–1978* (New York: W. W. Norton, 1979), 39.

11. Suzanne Juhasz, *Naked and Fiery Forms* (New York: Octagon, 1976), 4.

12. Carolyn Burke, "Supposed Persons: Modernist Poetry and the Female Subject," *Feminist Studies* 2, no. 1 (Spring 1985): 131, 141. In "Getting Spliced: Modernism and Sexual Difference," Burke associates Moore's particular collage methods with the "asexual" (*American Quarterly* 39, no. 1 [Spring 1987], 115).

13. For an account of the many ways that women writers and their work have been pejoratively stereotyped, see Alicia Ostriker, *Stealing the Language: The Emergence of Women's Poetry in America* (Boston: Beacon Press, 1986), 1–6.

14. See, for example, Irigaray, especially 148–150; and Susan Winnett, "Coming Unstrung: Women, Men, Narrative, and Principles of Pleasure," *PMLA* 105, no. 3 (May 1990): 505–518.

15. Myra Jehlen poses the question of how a criticism that addresses the ways we conceive of men and women is to establish itself, since the very terms of its discussion are undergoing redefinition. She compares the problem to that of Archimedes "who to lift the earth with his lever requires some place on which to locate himself and his fulcrum." Jehlen advocates a radical comparativism between men's and women's writing and establishes the border between them, a "no man's land," as a place where the feminist critic might stand ("Archimedes and the Paradox of Feminist Criticism," *Signs* 6, no. 4 [Summer 1981]: 575–601.)

16. Simone De Beauvoir stresses that men can assume a universal position, but

women are always marked by their gender, as the "Other" (*The Second Sex* [New York: Vintage Books, 1952] xv–xxxiv).

17. I have taken the concept of writing "in drag" from Margaret Homans', "Syllables of Velvet: Dickinson, Rossetti, and the Rhetorics of Sexuality," *Feminist Studies* 2, no. 3 (Fall 1985): 569–593.

18. Lawrence Lipking suggests that the figure of the abandoned woman is crucial to both men's and women's poetry (*Abandoned Women and Poetic Tradition* [Chicago: University of Chicago Press, 1988]). Adrienne Rich early on in her career noted the limitations of a woman's poetry that was primarily a poetry of complaint or of the "blues" ("When We Dead Awaken: Writing as Re-Vision").

19. Irigaray makes a similar distinction: "Speaking (as) woman is not speaking of woman. It is not a matter of producing a discourse of which woman would be the object, or the subject. . . . That said, by *speaking (as) woman*, one may attempt to provide a place for the 'other' as feminine" (135).

20. Irigaray uses the term "self-affection" throughout *This Sex Which Is Not One* (see especially 132–133).

21. Moore, in an undated letter from 1907 wrote, "I intend to write a light essay on the futility of introspection" (Rosenbach, [VI:13a:01]). The phrase "'business documents and school books'" is taken from her poem "Poetry," *Observations*, 31.

22. Nancy K. Miller in her essay, "Emphasis Added: Plots and Plausibilities in Women's Fiction," makes reference to Genette's concept of "plausible" silence, as a tacit contract between a work and its public (*PMLA* 96, no. 1 [January 1981]: 38). The phrase "Pleasure . . . out of sight" belongs to Samuel Butler, quoted by Moore (*Complete Prose*, 34).

23. "One need not know the way to be arriving" is from Moore's early poem "To a Man Working His Way Through a Crowd" (*Egoist* 2 [April 1915]: 62); "an avowed artist . . . must be an artist in refusing" is in Moore's *Complete Prose* (161); "in magnetism the potent factor is reserve" is from her early, unpublished review of *Casuals of the Sea* by William McFee, Rosenbach (II:01:24); and "omissions are not accidents" serves as an epigraph to *The Complete Poems*.

24. Pierre Macherey, *A Theory of Literary Production*, trans. Geoffrey Wall (London: Routledge & Kegan Paul, 1978), 41, 80, 84, 93–94, 101.

25. Macherey, 87, 199.

26. Janet Wolf, *The Social Production of Art* (London: Macmillan, 1981), 132.

27. Jacques Lacan, "God and the *Jouissance* of the Woman," in *Feminine Sexuality: Jacques Lacan and the école freudienne*, eds. Juliet Mitchell and Jacqueline Rose (New York: Norton, 1982), 144.

28. Irigaray, 30, 68–85, 80.

29. Although the terms symbolic and specular are not interchangeable, they are related. A traditional literary symbolism might well be seen as an intensification of the inherently specular propensities of discourse as established by Irigaray or as a conflation of Lacan's imaginary and symbolic functions.

30. Two feminist critics have made central use of Irigaray's theories in considering differences between men's and women's poetry: Jan Montefiore, in her *Feminism and Poetry* (New York: Pandora, 1987) and Margaret Homans, in her "Syllables of

Velvet." While Montefiore provides a detailed discussion of the relationship of the "I-Thou" in the mirror stage and in lyric poetry, her search to identify a female imaginary that would somehow supercede women's alienation in the Lacanian symbolic order is misguided. As she herself ultimately concludes, "A poetry of purely feminine identity is not, then, a really viable possibility, whether it is imagined in the language of radical feminism or in Irigaray's post-Lacanian terms . . . [the] struggle to transform inherited meanings is where the real strength and specificity of women's poetry lies" (179). Homans notes that in lyric poetry "underwriting both the plot of male desire and the plot of metaphor is a hierarchical power structure implicit in both, a hierarchy that permits one term—whether the romantic (male) subject or one term of a metaphor—to claim the authority to define the other— whether the feminine object of romantic desire or the second term of a metaphor" (573). For Homans, women poets can evade their transcription in this economy, at least in part, through a metonymic use of language.

31. Irigaray, 108.

32. Moore, *Complete Prose*, 431.

33. Moore, in her essay "Histrionic Seclusion," writes about the pleasure of "resolving a promised climax into contradiction" (*Complete Prose*, 108). In her essay "A Modest Expert" she writes, "tentativeness can be more positive than positiveness" (*Complete Prose*, 408). "The final . . . truth" is from her essay "Well Moused, Lion" (*Complete Prose*, 91).

34. T. S. Eliot, "Hamlet," in *Selected Prose of T. S. Eliot*, ed. Frank Kermode (New York: Harcourt Brace Jovanovich, 1975), 48.

35. Moore, *Complete Prose*, 420.

36. Frederic Jameson, *The Political Unconscious: Narrative as a Socially Symbolic Act* (Ithaca, New York: Cornell University Press, 1985), 214, 225, 236–237.

37. Charles Altieri stresses the achievement of Modernist art in its rejection of a mimetic or representational art for one that "must be abstract." Abstract art can reflect on its "compositional energies by which art both revels in its own abundance and makes that abundance a vehicle for defining fresh dimensions of its subject" (*Painterly Abstraction in Modernist American Poetry: The Contemporaneity of Modernism* [Cambridge: Cambridge University Press, 1989], 15). Alice Jardine comments on the process of "gynesis," in which such leading male theorists as Derrida and DeLeuze, among others, are involved in deconstructing the place of woman as other (*Gynesis: Configurations of Woman and Modernity* [Ithaca: Cornell University Press, 1985]).

38. Goodridge comments that Moore shared "a strong sense of the importance of [the Modernist's] collective critical mission." She elaborates, "As we conceive of the canons today we forget how much the public as well as the private exchanges these writers had with one another about each other's work linked them to a common enterprise" (6).

39. Rachel Du Plessis overemphasizes Moore's commitment to a "provisional" or "skeptical" writing given her equally strong impulses to "harmony" and "truth" ("No More of the Same: The Feminist Poetics of Marianne Moore," *William Carlos Williams Review* 14, no. 1 [Spring 1988]: 6–32).

40. Moore, *Complete Prose*, 177.

41. The comment on Stevens is from Moore, *Complete Prose*, 93. The remark about

Williams is from Moore's June 22, 1951 letter to him (Rosenbach [V: 77: 25]), quoted in Goodridge, 77.

42. Moore, *Complete Prose*, 272.

43. Moore, *Complete Prose*, 39.

44. Quoted in Kalstone, 90, from Elizabeth Bishop, *The Collected Prose*, 146–147.

45. Moore, *Complete Prose*, 8.

46. Moore, *Complete Prose*, 398.

47. Jarrell (See Chapter 1, n. 8).

CHAPTER 2

1. Moore, *Complete Prose*, 328.

2. Moore, *Complete Prose*, 177.

3. Bonnie Costello, *Marianne Moore: Imaginary Possessions* (Cambridge: Harvard University Press, 1981), 4. Although Costello does not specifically attribute Moore's non-possessive relationship to others to her position in the larger culture as a woman, many of her comments in their emphasis on Moore's refusal of singular definitions and identities bear out my claims that Moore writes from "elsewhere."

4. Kenner, "Disliking It," 117.

5. Pound's "Portrait d'une Femme" was published in 1912; Eliot's "Portrait of a Lady" appeared in 1917, a few months before Moore's "Those Various Scalpels."

6. Moore, *Complete Prose*, 35.

7. Nancy Vickers, "Diana Described: Scattered Woman and Scattered Rhyme," in *Writing and Sexual Difference*, ed. Elizabeth Abel (Chicago: University of Chicago Press, 1982) 102, 106. Vickers is quoting Josette Feral, "Antigone or *The Irony of the Tribe*," trans. Alice Jardine and Tom Gora, *Diacritics* 8 (Fall 1978): 7.

8. Ezra Pound, "Portrait d'une Femme," in *Personae* (New York: New Directions, 1971), 61.

9. T. S. Eliot, "Hamlet," in *Selected Prose*, 48–49.

10. T. S. Eliot, "Portrait of a Lady," in *Collected Poems* (New York: Harcourt Brace Jovanovich, 1970), 8–12.

11. William Carlos Williams, "Portrait of a Lady," in *Selected Poems* (New York: New Directions, 1969), 33–34.

12. In a discussion of this poem at the Marianne Moore Centennial Conference, Orono, Maine, 1987, the range of possible identities for the entity in "Those Various Scalpels" was truly various: a twentieth-century femme fatale with her knives (nails) on display, a woman warrior, an Athena, a symbol of the patriarchal state, and a sixteenth- or seventeenth-century knight or soldier. While many critics assume the figure to be a woman, there is nothing in the poem to warrant such an assumption. Carolyn Burke in "Getting Spliced: Modernism and Sexual Difference" suggests that Mina Loy may have inspired the poem.

13. Kenner, "Disliking It," 101.

14. Margaret Homans, "Representation, Reproduction, and Women's Place in Language," in *Bearing the Word: Language and Female Experience in Nineteenth-Century*

Women's Writing (Chicago: University of Chicago Press, 1968), 1–39. Nancy Chodorow, *The Reproduction of Mothering: Psychoanalysis and the Sociology of Gender* (Berkeley: University of California Press, 1978).

15. Eliot, "Marianne Moore (1923)," 49.

16. Mark Van Doren, "Women of Wit," *The Nation* 113, no. 2938 (26 October 1921): 482.

17. Jarrell (see Chapter 1, n. 8).

18. Shari Benstock, *Women of the Left Bank* (Austin: University of Texas Press, 1986), 26. Benstock is quoting Susan Stanford Friedman, *Psyche Reborn: The Emergence of H. D.* (Bloomington: Indiana University Press, 1981), 97. See also, Sandra Gilbert and Susan Gubar, *No Man's Land: The Place of Women Writers in the Twentieth Century* Vols. 1–2 (New Haven, Connecticut: Yale University Press, 1988).

19. Pound, "Three Cantos," *Poetry* 10, no. 5 (August 1917): 250.

20. Eliot, "The Love Song of J. Alfred Prufrock," *Collected Poems*, 3–7.

21. Pound, "Hugh Selwyn Mauberly," *Personae*, 203–204.

22. Pound, "Hugh Selwyn Mauberly," *Personae*, 201.

23. Moore, "No Swan So Fine," *Selected Poems*, 31.

24. Moore uses the word "miscellany" frequently in her prose. For a prose piece in praise of the miscellany in anthologies, see *Complete Prose*, 182–184.

25. Moore, "When I Buy Pictures," *Observations*, 59.

CHAPTER 3

1. Ezra Pound, *The Spirit of Romance* (Norfolk, Connecticut: J. Laughlin, 1952), 87, 94.

2. Moore to family, 11 February 1908, Rosenbach, (VI: 14:03).

3. See Introduction, n. 12.

4. For example, T. S. Eliot remarks in his introduction to Moore's *Selected Poems*, "So far back as my memory extends . . . Miss Moore has no poetic derivations. I cannot, therefore, fill up my pages with the usual account of influences and development" (6–7). In his essay "Disliking It," Hugh Kenner comments, "Miss Moore's modest effort was not to deflect poetry, or to destroy it, but to ignore it" (109). More recently, John Slatin, in *The Savage's Romance*, has argued that in the first part of her career Moore willfully refused to acknowledge her indebtedness to the literary tradition, although she eventually came to do so. In *An Enabling Humility*, Jeredith Merrin claims the opposite, suggesting that Moore from the very beginning of her career was strongly influenced by Renaissance Protestant sources, such as Sir Thomas Browne and George Herbert (New Brunswick, New Jersey: Rutgers University Press, 1990).

5. Hall, "An Interview," 17.

6. See Chapter 1, n. 18.

7. See Introduction, n. 13.

8. Alicia Ostriker uses the term "duplicitous" to describe the poetic doubleness of women poets whose poetry means what it says and also its opposite (*Stealing the Language*, 37–41).

9. Todorov, *The Fantastic*, 35.

10. Brooke-Rose, *A Rhetoric of the Unreal*, 3–11, 55–71.

11. In addition to poems listed here, see Moore, "Holes Bored in a Workbag by the Scissors," *Bruno's Weekly*, 7 October 1916: 1137, and "To An Intramural Rat," *Observations*, 9.

12. Moore, "He did mend it . . . ," unpublished poem, Rosenbach, (I:02:17).

13. Moore, "Diligence Is to Magic as Progress Is to Flight," *Observations*, 22. All subsequent poems in this chapter are from *Observations*, unless otherwise noted.

14. Moore to family, 28 February 1908, Rosenbach, (VI:14:03).

15. These criticisms appear in letters by Moore, dated 19 February 1907 and 25 February 1907, (both VI:13a:03); 3 February 1908, (VI:14:03); 18 March 1908, (VI:14:04); and 3 March 1909, (VI:15a:04) (Rosenbach).

16. Moore to family, 20 February 1908, (VI:14:03); 24 October 1907, (VI:13b:ll); and 14 February 1909, (VI:15a:03) (Rosenbach).

17. Moore to family, 19 March 1908, Rosenbach, (VI:14:04).

18. The term "byplay" occurs in Moore's poem "In This Age of Hard Trying Nonchalance Is Good And" (*Observations*, 28). In her unpublished prose piece, "Melodrama," Moore comments, "Turgenef's most striking narrative byplay is melodramatic in character" (Rosenbach [II:04:12]).

19. Moore, "Things Are What They Seem," *Lantern* 21 (Spring 1913): 109.

20. Moore, "My Senses Do Not Deceive Me," *Lantern* 18 (Spring 1910): 103.

21. Mary Nearing, "A Sonnet," *Tipyn O'Bob* 5 (November 1907): 12.

22. Moore, "To Come After a Sonnet," *Tipyn O'Bob* 5 (November 1907): 25. Reprinted in *Marianne Moore Newsletter* 5, no. 1 (Spring 1981): 17.

23. Moore, "Progress," *Tipyn O'Bob* 6 (June 1909): 10. This poem was not published in any of Moore's volumes of poetry until 1967 in her *Complete Poems*, and then under the title, "I May, I Might, I Must" (178).

24. Moore to family, 4 Feb. 1909, Rosenbach, (VI:15a:03).

25. Moore, "To My Cup-Bearer," *Tipyn O'Bob* 5 (April 1908): 21. Reprinted in *Marianne Moore Newsletter* 5, no. 1 (Spring 1981): 17.

26. Moore, "Diogenes," *Contemporary Verse* 1 (January 1916): 6.

27. Quoted in Stapleton, 36. Stapleton is quoting a letter from Moore to Scofield Thayer, 2 Sept. 1924, Beinecke Library, Yale University Library. The second quotation is from Moore's essay, "Humility, Concentration, and Gusto," *The Complete Prose*, 420.

28. For a fine discussion of the dialectical processes at work in "Critics and Connoisseurs," see Schulman, 50–54. Schulman, however, maintains that Moore ultimately elects "conscious fastidiousness" over "unconscious fastidiousness."

29. Molesworth, xvii, 144.

30. Molesworth 92, 123, 137, 229, 230, and 272.

31. Costello notes that the "they" might be a larger public (*Imaginary Possessions*, 31).

32. Moore, "Blake," *Others*, 1, no. 6 (Dec. 1915): 105.

33. Moore, manuscript of "Injudicious Gardening," Rosenbach, (I:02:38).

34. Molesworth, 49.

35. Stapleton, 13.

36. Sandra Gilbert and Susan Gubar, *The Madwoman in the Attic* (New Haven, Connecticut: Yale University Press, 1980) 45–92.

37. Moore, "To William Butler Yeats on Tagore," *Poems*, 8.

38. Moore, "To a Man Working His Way Through a Crowd," *The Egoist* 2, no. 4 (April 1915): 62.

39. "Unspells" appears in Moore's poem, "To a Man Working His Way Through a Crowd," *The Egoist* 2, no. 4 (April 1915): 62. "Come / At the cause of the shouts" is from Moore's "The Past Is the Present, in *Others: An Anthology of the New Verse*, ed. Alfred Kreymborg (New York: Alfred A. Knopf, 1917), 74–75. This poem shares only the title with the better known 1915 poem.

40. In her notebook, Moore copied many pages of notes from Turgenev's *Fathers and Sons* and *Rudin* (Rosenbach [VII:01:01]).

41. Ostriker, *Stealing the Language*, 82–85.

42. Quoted in "Prince Rupert's Drop," *Marianne Moore Newsletter* 1, no. 2 (Fall 1977): 11.

43. Quoted in Costello, *Imaginary Possessions*, 48.

44. Robert Pinsky, "Marianne Moore: Idiom and Idiosyncrasy," in Parisi, *The Art of a Modernist*, 14.

45. Thomas Hardy, *A Pair of Blue Eyes*, (New York: Harper and Brothers, 1905), 171–174. For identifying the Hardy novel and similarities among these three early poems, I am indebted to Patricia Willis, "MM, Hardy, and Critics," *Marianne Moore Newsletter* 2, no. 2 (Fall 1978): 7–10.

46. Moore paraphrases the Dean's assessment of one of her stories as "It was a pity a girl of such ability should be guilty of such affectations . . . the kind of thing in this story . . . was the kind of thing that makes the college ridiculous to outsiders." Letter to family, 14 April 1908, Rosenbach, (VI:14:05). The phrase "unashamedly . . . real" is from Moore's letter to family, 20 February 1908, Rosenbach, (VI:14:03).

47. Molesworth, 225.

48. Moore, "My Lantern," *Lantern* 18 (Spring 1910): 28.

49. Quoted in Willis, "MM, Hardy, and Critics," 9.

50. Slatin, *The Savage's Romance*, 36–37.

51. Moore, "In This Age of Hard Trying Nonchalance Is Good And," *Observations*, 28.

52. Hélène Cixous, "The Laugh of the Medusa," trans. Keith and Paula Cohen, in *New French Feminisms*, eds. Elaine Marks and Isabelle de Courtivon (Amherst: The University of Massachusetts Press, 1980), 245–264.

CHAPTER 4

1. Moore, review of *A Metropolitan Hermit* by Stewart Mitchell, in *Complete Prose*, 62.

2. William Carlos Williams, "Marianne Moore (1925)," in *Marianne Moore: A Collection of Critical Essays*, ed. Charles Tomlinson (Englewood Cliffs, New Jersey: Prentice-Hall, 1969), 58.

3. See Introduction, n. 12.

4. All of Moore's poems in this chapter are taken from *Observations*, unless otherwise noted.

5. Eleven different published versions of "Poetry" have been counted. Patricia C. Willis and Clive E. Driver account for nine in "Bibliographic Numbering and Marianne Moore" (*PBSA* 70 [1976]: 261–263). Jeffrey D. Peterson establishes two more in "Notes on the Poem(s) 'Poetry': The Ingenuity of Moore's Poetic 'Place,'" in *Marianne Moore: Woman and Poet*, ed. Patricia C. Willis (Orono: National Poetry Foundation, 1991), 223–242.

6. In her 1963 interview with Donald Hall, Moore explained her extensive use of quotations as motivated by a desire "to be honorable and not to steal things. I've always felt that if a thing has been said in the very best way, how can you say it better" (Hall, "An Inteview," 30).

7. Moore, "Poe, Byron, and Bacon," unpublished prose, Rosenbach, (II:05:08).

8. Moore, "Edgar Poe: A Portrait in Gold Thread," unpublished poetry, Rosenbach, (I:01:38).

9. Moore, "Poe, Byron, and Bacon," Rosenbach, (II:05:08).

10. Moore, "The Accented Syllable," *Complete Prose*, 32–33. Because of its more critical attitude toward Poe, I assume, but have not established, that this article was written later in 1916 than "Poe, Byron, and Bacon."

11. Wallace Stevens, "The Noble Rider and the Sound of Words," *The Necessary Angel* (New York: Alfred A. Knopf, 1951), 36. In two reviews of Stevens' work, Moore praises him for his imaginative "evasions" (*Complete Prose*, 91, 330).

12. Moore, review of *Casuals of the Sea*, Rosenbach, (II:01:24).

13. Moore, review of *Three Soldiers* by John Dos Passos, Rosenbach, (II:06:18).

14. Williams, "Marianne Moore (1925)," in *Marianne Moore*, ed. Charles Tomlinson, 53.

15. Moore, "An Octopus," *Observations*, 83, 90.

16. Slatin links Moore's change from syllabic to free verse forms in 1921–25 to her shift away from what he describes as her "isolationist tendencies." However, he does not explain why in her later poetry, in which she is presumably even less of an "isolationist," she reverts to syllabics (see *Savage's Romance*, especially 3–4).

17. See, for instance, Slatin, *Savage's Romance*, 95.

18. Nestor, *The Greek Anthology*, trans. W. R. Paton, 5 vols. (Cambridge: Harvard University Press, 1958), 3: 67. Although in her note Moore lists p. 129, the reference is to entry 129.

19. Stapleton (18–19) cites a version published in *Lantern* in 1919:

    In the shortlegged, fit-
ful advance, in the gurglings and all the minutiae, we have the classic
multitude of feet—formidable only in the
    dark. Truth, many legged and formidable also,
is stationary by choice.
    The wave may go over it if it likes; know

that it will be there when it says: I shall be
there when the wave has gone by.

20. Costello comments on the concluding lines, "The quotation marks a difference, but the words mark an identity. We have at once the illusion of truth's presence
and the awareness of a proxy" (*Imaginary Possessions*, 28).

21. Stapleton, 19.

22. See Chapter 3, n. 41.

23. Costello, *Imaginary Possessions*, 2.

24. Slatin, *Savage's Romance*, 40–58.

25. Costello poses the question of whether the genuine is "stimulus" or "response" (*Imaginary Possessions*, 20).

26. Slatin, *Savage's Romance*, 43.

27. Slatin stresses that Moore has no quarrel with Yeats' description of Blake,
only with his valuation (*Savage's Romance*, 53–54).

28. Teresa de Lauretis, *Alice Doesn't: Feminism, Semiotics, Cinema* (Bloomington: Indiana University Press, 1984), 12–36.

29. Stapleton remarks that the mood of the poem is affected by Moore's "feelings
about the first World War and her brother's willing assumption of the dangers inherent in naval service" (20). My observations concerning suicide are based on the
poem itself. In "Is Your Town Nineveh?" and "Feed Me, Also, River God" (both
1916), Moore atypically explores feelings of despair (*Observations*, 17 and *Poems*, 8).
Moore finished at least one version of "A Grave," originally titled "A Graveyard," by
1918, but did not publish it until 1921.

30. M. H. Abrams, "Structure and Style in the Greater Romantic Lyric," in *Romanticism and Consciousness*, ed. Harold Bloom (New York: Norton, 1970), 201–229.

31. Merrin also comments on how "A Grave" is working within and against a
Romantic tradition (*An Enabling Humility*, 61–80).

32. For an account of Moore's correspondence with Pound regarding "A Grave,"
see Stapleton, 21–25.

33. In a review of Moore's *Complete Poems*, Ashbery comments that Moore's mind
always "moves in a straight line, [but it] does so over a terrain that is far from level"
(quoted in Molesworth, 443–444).

34. Williams, "Marianne Moore (1925)," *Marianne Moore*, 54.

35. Moore, "When I Buy Pictures," *The Dial* 71 (July 1921): 33.

36. Moore, "When I Buy Pictures," *Poems*, 17.

37. Quoted in Stapleton, 237. The comment is taken from Henry Osborn Tay-
lor's *The Medieval Mind*, as recorded by Moore in one of her notebooks (Rosenbach
[VII: 01:02]).

38. Moore expressed approval of Eliot's distinction between "brillance of surface
and mere superificiality," quoting his remark about Ben Jonson, " 'The superficies is
the world' " (*Complete Prose*, 54).

39. Slatin, *Savage's Romance*, 127–136.

40. Costello, *Imaginary Possessions*, 173.

41. Goodridge focuses her entire book on Moore's relationship to Williams,

Eliot, Stevens, and Pound, asserting that Moore frequently makes, but hides, critical remarks about her contemporaries.

42. Moore, *Complete Prose*, 431.

43. See, for example, Moore's "To a Chameleon" (1916), *Observations*, 11, and "The Plumet Basilisk" (1933), *Selected Poems*, 32–37. The term "intermittent" appears in "The Plumet Basilisk."

44. I am using the term "mimic," as Luce Irigaray defines and uses it in *This Sex Which Is Not One*, 76–77.

CHAPTER 5

1. Kate Greenaway, "The king said," quoted in Moore, *Complete Prose*, 154.

2. Moore, *Complete Prose*, 183.

3. "Hybrid method," quoted in Stapleton, 49. "Said in the very best way," quoted in Hall, "An Interview," 30.

4. Blackmur, 83.

5. "People's Surroundings" was first published in *The Dial*, June 1922. *The Wasteland* came out simultaneously in *The Dial* and *The Criterion* in October 1922.

6. Goodridge comments on Moore's critical silence regarding *The Wasteland*, suggesting that Moore may have not written on *The Wasteland* because its rapid ascendancy meant that her critical advocacy was not needed. She also speculates that Moore may have had her reservations about Eliot's poetry, because its "'romantic' journey toward the self and its frustrations was much too direct" (133).

7. Blackmur, 85.

8. Kenner, "Disliking It," in *A Homemade World*, 102.

9. Irigaray criticizes the "structuration of (the) language" for its "complicity of long standing between rationality and a mechanics of solids" (107). All poems by Moore quoted in this chapter are taken from *Observations*, unless otherwise noted.

10. Irigaray 106, 107.

11. See, for example, "Wet Casements," *Houseboat Days* (New York: Viking, 1977), 28.

12. See especially Homans, *Women Writers and Poetic Identity: Dorothy Wordsworth, Emily Bronte, and Emily Dickinson* (Princeton: Princeton University Press, 1980) and *Bearing the Word*.

13. Moore, Rosenbach, (VII:04:04), and all subsequent references to Moore's notebook.

14. The first of the two passages was brought to my attention by Patricia C. Willis, "The Road to Paradise: First Notes on Marianne Moore's 'An Octopus,'" *Twentieth Century Literature* 30, nos. 2–3 (Summer-Fall 1984): 247.

15. Much current feminist film criticism concerned with audience response focuses on the kinds of identifications cinema affords. By emphasizing strategies for disrupting the "natural," "male gaze" of the camera, feminist art risks losing one of the most powerful aspects of the cinema, namely its capacity to involve audiences in identificatory processes. By juxtaposing diverse images and phrases, Moore, like the feminist filmmaker Yvonne Rainier, is able to engage her audience in limited and circumscribed forms of identification. For feminist film critics who address this

problem, see Laura Mulvey, "Visual Pleasure and Narrative Cinema," *Screen* 16, no. 3 (Autumn 1975): 6–18; Teresa De Lauretis, "Oedipus Interruptus," *Wide Angle* 7, nos. 1–2 (1985): 34–40; and Yvonne Rainier, "More Kicking and Screaming from the Narrative Front/Backwater," *Wide Angle* 7, nos. 1–2 (1985): 8–12.

16. Quoted in Stapleton, 36. The 2 September 1924 letter from which Stapleton quotes is part of Moore's correspondence to Scofield Thayer housed in the Beinecke Library at Yale University.

17. Quoted in Stapleton, 37. The 18 March 1923 letter is in the Rosenbach, (VI: 26: 04).

18. Stapleton remarks that the "brilliance" of "Marriage" "is set off by a faceting that prevents the reader from looking at the center of poetic energy" (40).

19. Ostriker claims that "Marriage" "hides—under its elliptical surface—a rather absolute critique of patriarchy and its central institution" (*Stealing the Language*, 51). Lynn Keller and Cristanne Miller in "'the tooth of disputation:' Marianne Moore's 'Marriage," emphasize the "poet's deep ambivalence about the 'enterprise,' of marriage" (*Sagetrieb* 6, no. 3 [Winter 1987]: 100).

20. Stapleton remarks that Eve "in her various guises . . . remains 'the central flaw / in that first crystal fine experiment'" (38). Keller and Miller maintain that "despite Moore's slightly more favorable portrait of the 'She,' both characters are repugnant in their viciousness and both are explicitly condemned for loving themselves too much" (110).

21. Milton, John, "Paradise Lost," *Complete Poems and Major Prose*, ed. Merritt Y. Hughes (Indianapolis: Odyssey Press, 1957), Chapter 4, lines 440–443.

22. Milton, Chapter 8, lines 270–273.

23. Milton, Chapter 4, lines 449–469, 475–480. Christine Froula claims that Eve is remembering an "origin innocent of patriarchal indoctrination, one whose resonances the covering trope of narcissism does not entirely suffice to control" ("When Eve Reads Milton: Undoing the Canonical Economy," *Critical Inquiry* 10 no. 2 [December 1983]: 321–347)

24. In some versions of the myth Philomela is turned into a swallow and Procne into a nightingale. Edward Tripp, *The Meridian Handbook of Classical Mythology* (New York: New American Library, 1970), 552–553.

25. Edward Thomas, *Feminine Influence on the Poets* (New York: John Lane Company, 1911), 110–111.

26. Stapleton notes that a number of Moore's and Thayer's friends thought that Thayer wished to marry Moore and quotes Moore as describing the news of Bryhers' marriage as "an earthquake" (41). Keller and Miller document a possible proposal of marriage to Moore from Scofield Thayer and her conflicting attitudes toward the marriage of Bryher and Robert McAlmon (110). In 1918 Moore's brother, Warner, married against his mother's wishes, an event which shook the emotionally close family (Molesworth, 132–133).

27. Willis, "The Road to Paradise," 249.

28. Willis, "The Road to Paradise," 251.

29. See Introduction, n. 12.

30. Patrocinio P. Schweickart comments on "[the] denigration of female difference into otherness without reciprocity," as an effect of universalizing (masculine)

texts ("Reading Ourselves: Toward a Feminist Theory of Reading," in *Gender and Reading*, eds. Elizabeth Flynn and Patrocinio P. Schweickart [Baltimore: The Johns Hopkins Press, 1986], 42).

31. Montefiore, 103–104.

CHAPTER 6

1. Pound, "How to Read," in *Literary Essays of Ezra Pound*, ed. T. S. Eliot (New York: New Directions, 1935), 27.

2. Moore, *Complete Prose*, 214–215.

3. See Introduction, n. 16.

4. Marie Borroff, *Language and the Poet* (Chicago: University of Chicago Press, 1979), 82–83.

5. Borroff maintains that the writings and teaching of the Christian church were a major influence on the poetry of Moore, Stevens, and Frost (3).

6. Molesworth, 272.

7. Molesworth, 259–260.

8. Molesworth, 265.

9. Kalstone, 101.

10. Quoted in Stapleton, 188.

11. Molesworth, 247.

12. 7 March 1937 letter to Bishop, quoted in Bonnie Costello, "Marianne Moore and Elizabeth Bishop," 139.

13. Moore to family, 19 March 1908, Rosenbach, (VI: 14:04).

14. Moore, "Black Earth," *Observations*, 45–47.

15. Moore, "Elephants," *Nevertheless* (New York: Macmillan, 1944), 4–6.

16. Moore, "Spenser's Ireland," in *What Are Years* (New York: Macmillan, 1941), 34–36.

17. Lisa Steinman comments that Moore attempts to redefine and revalue such aspects of a technological and industrial America as "science, fact, accuracy, speed, and the vocabulary of profit" (130). She establishes Moore's motivation to defend these attributes, as based in part on her rejection of large generalizing statements condemning technological advancement by such critics as Lewis Mumford, who maintained that America's material success was a symptom of its spiritual failure. Steinman, however, criticizes the lack of comprehensiveness of Moore's perspective:

> Her ultimate insistence on the primacy of the individual mind's confrontations with its world may have prevented her from going on to offer analyses of such questions as why women as a class might be served by technological advances or why certain character traits are fostered by postindustrial societies. Moreover, the valorization of speed and efficiency as imaginative virtues may have masked the need to question such values in other spheres; one must recall that as Moore wrote, efficiency became the battle cry of American business, inspired by Taylorism, and so was a bone of contention between labor and management" ("Marianne Moore: The Anaconda-Like Curves of Central Bearings," in *Made in America: Science, Technology and American Modernist Poetics* [New Haven, Connecticut: Yale University Press, 1987] 113–132.)

18. "Bell Telephone Laboratories" is in "Four Quartz Crystal Clocks," (*What Are Years*, 37–38); "The John Day Company" and "the bock-beer buck" appear in "Armour's Undermining Modesty (*The Collected Poems* [New York: Macmillan, 1951], 149, 176); and the "taslon shirt" is in "Saint Nicholas" (*O to Be a Dragon*, 25–26).

19. For a more detailed discussion of Moore's earlier poems, see preceding chapters.

20. Moore, "The Mind Is an Enchanting Thing," in *Nevertheless* (New York: Macmillan, 1951), 10–11.

21. Moore, "What Are Years?," *What Are Years*, 1; "In Distrust of Merits," *Nevertheless*, 12–14; "Keeping Their World Large," *Collected Poems*, 144–145.

22. Moore, "Propriety," *Collected Poems*, 147–148.

23. Moore, "The Jerboa," *Selected Poems*, 22–27; "The Frigate Pelican," *Selected Poems*, 38–41; "The Plumet Basilisk," *Selected Poems*, 32.

24. For a discussion of these terms, see Chapter 1.

25. For a discussion of these ideas, see Chapter 1.

26. Moore, "Bird-Witted," *The Pangolin and Other Verse* (London: The Brendin Publishing Company, 1936), 10–11; "He 'Digesteth Harde Yron,'" *What Are Years*, 6–9; "A Carriage From Sweden," *Nevertheless*, 7–9; "The Arctic Ox (or Goat)," *O to Be a Dragon*, 22–23.

27. See Chapter 1, n. 37.

28. In a 1934 letter to her brother in which she mentions receiving the contract from Faber and Faber for her *Selected Poems*, she signed the letter "Rat," with the "A" in red, adding "hereinafter called Author" (Molesworth, 266). See also Molesworth 25–26, 106, and 128–129.

29. Molesworth, 258.

30. "Virginia Britannica," *The Pangolin*, 3–9.

31. "Half-Deity," *The Pangolin*, 12–14.

32. "Pigeons," *Poetry* 47, no. 2 (Nov. 1935): 61–65.

33. Moore, Rosenbach, (VII: 04: 04).

34. Costello, *Imaginary Possessions*, 149, 147. Costello takes her description of the basilisk from Jorge Luis Borges, *Book of Imaginary Beings*.

35. Molesworth, 278, 304.

AFTERWORD

1. Macherey, 84.

2. Irigaray, 30.

3. Kenner, "Disliking It," 117.

4. Helen Vendler, "Marianne Moore," *Part of Nature; Part of Us* (Cambridge: Harvard University Press, 1980), 69.

5. Rachel Du Plessis, *H. D.* (Bloomington: Indiana University Press, 1986) 16–17.

6. For example, H. D. concludes *Trilogy* with an innocent Mary who is seen through the perspective of the wise, male Kaspar:

But she spoke so he looked at her,
she was shy and simple and young;

she said, Sir, it is a most beautiful fragrance,
as of all flowering things together;

but Kaspar knew the seal of the jar was unbroken
he did not know whether she knew

the fragrance came from the bundle of myrrh
she held in her arms.

(H. D., *Collected Poems*, ed. Louis Martz [New York: New Directions, 1983], 612.)

 7. Gertrude Stein, *The Yale Gertrude Stein*, ed. Richard Kostelantz (New Haven, Connecticut: Yale University Press, 1980), xix, xxii.

SELECTED BIBLIOGRAPHY

Abbott, Craig. *Marianne Moore: A Descriptive Bibliography*. Pittsburgh: University of Pittsburgh Press, 1977.

Abel, Elizabeth, ed. *Writing and Sexual Difference*. Chicago: University of Chicago Press, 1982.

Abrams, M. H. "Structure and Style in the Greater Romantic Lyric." In *Romanticism and Consciousness*, ed. Harold Bloom, 201–229. New York: Norton, 1970.

Allen, Carolyn. "Feminist Criticism and Postmodernism." In *Tracing Literary Theory*, ed. Joseph Natoli, 278–305. Urbana, Illinois: University of Illinois Press, l987.

Althusser, Louis. *For Marx*. Trans. Ben Brewster. New York: Pantheon, 1969.

Altieri, Charles. *Act and Quality*. Amherst: The University of Massachusetts Press, 1981.

——. "Objective Image and Act of Mind in Modern Poetry." *PMLA* 91, no. 1 (January 1976): 110–114.

——. *Painterly Abstraction in Modernist American Poetry: The Contemporaneity of Modernism*. Cambridge: Cambridge University Press, 1989.

August, Bonnie Tymorski. *Womanhood in Five American Poets*. Ann Arbor: UMI, 1979.

Benstock, Shari. *Women of the Left Bank*. Austin: University of Texas Press, 1986.

Berg, Temma F., ed. *Engendering the Word: Feminist Essays in Psychosexual Poetics*. Urbana: University of Illinois Press, 1989.

Bishop, Elizabeth. "Efforts of Affection: A Memoir of Marianne Moore." In *The Collected Prose*, ed. Robert Giroux, 121–156. New York: Farrar Strauss Giroux, 1984.

Blackmur, R. P. "The Method of Marianne Moore." In *Marianne Moore: A Collection of Critical Essays*, ed. Charles Tomlinson, 66–86. Englewood Cliffs, New Jersey: Prentice-Hall, 1969.

Bloom, Harold, ed. *Modern Critical Views: Marianne Moore*. New York: Chelsea, 1987.

Borroff, Marie. *Language and the Poet*. Chicago: University of Chicago Press, 1979.

Brooke-Rose, Christine. *A Rhetoric of the Unreal*. London: Cambridge University Press, 1981.

Burke, Carolyn. "Getting Spliced: Modernism and Sexual Difference, *American Quarterly* 39, no. 1 (Spring 1987): 98–121.

————. "Supposed Persons: Modernist Poetry and the Female Subject." *Feminist Studies* 2, no. 1 (Spring 1985): 131–148.

Burke, Kenneth. "Motives and Motifs in the Poetry of Marianne Moore." In *Marianne Moore: A Collection of Critical Essays*, ed. Charles Tomlinson, 87–100. Englewood Cliffs, New Jersey: Prentice-Hall, 1969.

Chodorow, Nancy. *The Reproduction of Mothering: Psychoanalysis and the Sociology of Gender*. Berkeley: University of California Press, 1978.

Cixous, Hélène. "The Laugh of the Medusa," trans. Keith and Paul Cohen. In *New French Feminisms*, eds. Elaine Marks and Isabelle de Courtivon, 245–264. Amherst: The University of Massachuesetts Press, 1980.

Costello, Bonnie. "The 'Feminine' Language of Marianne Moore." In *Women and Language in Literature and Society*, eds. Sally McConnell-Ginet, Ruth Borker, and Nelly Furman, 222–238. New York: Praeger, 1980.

————. *Marianne Moore: Imaginary Possessions*. Cambridge: Harvard University Press, 1981.

————. "Marianne Moore and Elizabeth Bishop: Friendship and Influence." *Twentieth Century Literature* 30, nos. 2–3 (Summer-Fall 1984): 130–149.

Coward, Rosalind, and John Ellis. *Language and Materialism*. London: Routledge and Kegan Paul, 1977.

De Beauvoir, Simone. *The Second Sex*. New York: Vintage Books, 1952.

DeKoven, Marianne. *A Different Language: Gertrude Stein's Experimental Writing*. Madison: University of Wisconsin Press, 1983.

De Lauretis, Teresa. *Alice Doesn't: Feminism, Semiotics, Cinema*. Bloomington: Indiana University Press, 1984.

————. "Oedipus Interruptus." *Wide Angle* 7, nos. 1–2 (1985): 34–40.

Doane, Mary Ann. "Film and the Masquerade: Theorising the Female Spectator." *Screen* 23, nos. 3–4 (September–October 1982): 74–88.

Duncan, Robert. "Ideas of the Meaning of Form." In *Fictive Certainties*, 89–105. New York: New Directions, 1955.

Du Plessis, Rachel. *H. D.* Bloomington: Indiana University Press, 1986.

————. "No More of the Same: The Feminist Poetics of Marianne Moore." *William Carlos Williams Review* 14, no. 1 (Spring 1988): 6–32.

————. *Writing Beyond the Ending: Narrative Strategies of Twentieth-Century Women Writers*. Bloomington: Indiana University Press, 1985.

Eliot, T. S. *Collected Poems*. New York: Harcourt Brace Jovanovich, 1970.

————. Introduction to *Selected Poems*, by Marianne Moore, 5–12. New York: Macmillan, 1935.

————. "Marianne Moore (1923)" In *Marianne Moore: A Collection of Critical Essays*, ed. Charles Tomlinson, 48–51. Englewood Cliffs, New Jersey: Prentice-Hall, 1969.

————. *Selected Prose of T. S. Eliot*, ed. Frank Kermode. New York: Harcourt Brace Jovanovich, 1975.

Flynn, Elizabeth, and Patrocino P. Schweickart, eds. *Gender and Reading*. Baltimore: The Johns Hopkins University Press, 1986.

Foucault, Michel. *The History of Sexuality*. Trans. Robert Hurley. New York: Pantheon, 1978.

Friedman, Susan Stanford. *Psyche Reborn: The Emergence of H. D.* Bloomington: Indiana University Press, 1981.

Froula, Christine. "When Eve Reads Milton: Undoing the Canonical Economy." *Critical Inquiry* 10, no. 2 (December 1983): 321–347.

Gallagher, Tess. "Throwing the Scarecrows from the Garden." *Parnassus* 12, nos. 2–3 (1985): 45–60.

Garrigue, Jean. *Marianne Moore.* Minneapolis: University of Minnesota Press, 1965.

Gilbert, Sandra. "Marianne Moore as Female Female. Impersonator." In *Marianne Moore: The Art of a Modernist,* ed. Joseph Parisi, 27–46. Ann Arbor: University of Michigan Press, 1990.

Gilbert, Sandra, and Susan Gubar. *No Man's Land: The Place of the Woman Writer in the Twentieth Century* Vols. 1–2. New Haven, Connecticut: Yale University Press, 1988.

———. *The Madwoman in the Attic.* New Haven, Connecticut: Yale University Press, 1980.

———, eds. *Shakespeare's Sisters: Feminist Essays on Women Poets.* Bloomington: Indiana University Press, 1979.

Goodridge, Celeste. *Hints and Disguises: Marianne Moore and Her Contemporaries.* Iowa City: Iowa University Press, 1989.

Gregory, Elizabeth, "'Silence' and Restraint." In *Marianne Moore: Woman and Poet,* ed. Patricia C. Willis, 169–183. Orono: The National Poetry Foundation, 1991.

Hall, Donald. "The Art of Poetry: Marianne Moore. An Interview." In *Marianne Moore: A Critical Collection,* ed. Charles Tomlinson, 20–45. Englewood Cliffs, New Jersey: Prentice-Hall, 1969.

———. *Marianne Moore: The Cage and the Animal.* New York: Pegasus, 1970.

Hardy, Thomas. *A Pair of Blue Eyes.* New York: Harper and Brothers, 1905.

H. D. *Collected Poems,* ed. Louis Martz. New York: New Directions, 1983.

———. *Hermione.* 1927. Reprint. New York: New Directions, 1981.

———. *Notes on Thought and Vision.* Reprint. 1919. San Francisco: City Lights Books, 1982.

Heath, Stephen. "Difference." *Screen* 19, no. 3 (Autumn 1978): 51–112.

Hejinian, Lyn. "Two Stein Talks." *Temblor* 3 (1986): 128–139.

Holley, Margaret. "The Model Stanza: The Organic Origin of Moore's Syllabic Verse." *Twentieth Century Literature* 30, nos. 2–3 (Summer-Fall 1984): 181–191.

———. *The Poetry of Marianne Moore: A Study in Voice and Value.* Cambridge: Cambridge University Press, 1987.

Homans, Margaret. *Bearing the Word: Language and Female Experience in Nineteenth-Century Women's Writing.* Chicago: University of Chicago Press, 1968.

———. "Syllables of Velvet: Dickinson, Rossetti, and the Rhetorics of Sexuality." *Feminist Studies* 2, no. 3 (Fall 1985): 569–593.

———. *Women Writers and Poetic Identity: Dorothy Wordsworth, Emily Bronte, and Emily Dickinson.* Princeton: Princeton University Press, 1980.

Irigaray, Luce. *This Sex Which Is Not One,* trans. Catherine Porter. Ithaca, New York: Cornell University Press, 1985.

Jacobus, Mary. "The Question of Language: Men of Maxims and the Mill on the

Floss." In *Writing and Sexual Difference*, ed. Elizabeth Abel, 37–52. Chicago: University of Chicago Press, 1982.

Jameson, Frederic. "Imaginary and Symbolic in Lacan: Marxism, Psychoanalytic Criticism, and the Problem of the Subject." In *Literature and Psychoanalysis*, ed. Shoshana Felman, 339–395. Baltimore: Johns Hopkins University Press, 1982.

———. *The Political Unconscious: Narrative as a Socially Symbolic Act.* Ithaca, New York: Cornell University Press, 1981.

Jardine, Alice. *Gynesis: Configurations of Woman and Modernity.* Ithaca, New York: Cornell University Press, 1985.

Jarrell, Randall. "Her Shield." In *Marianne Moore: A Collection of Critical Essays*, ed. Charles Tomlinson, 114–124. Englewood Cliffs, New Jersey: Prentice-Hall, 1969.

Jehlen, Myra. "Archimedes and the Paradox of Feminist Criticism." *Signs* 6, no. 4 (Summer 1981): 575–601.

Jones, Ann Rosalind. "Assimilation with a Difference: Renaissance Women Poets and Literary Influence." *Yale French Studies* 62 (1981): 135–153.

Juhasz, Suzanne. *Naked and Fiery Forms.* New York: Octagon, 1976.

Kalstone, David. *Becoming a Poet: Elizabeth Bishop with Marianne Moore and Robert Lowell.* New York: Farrar Strauss Giroux, 1989.

Kammer, Jean. "The Art of Silence and the Forms of Women's Poetry." In *Shakespeare's Sisters: Feminist Essays on Women Poets*, eds. Sandra Gilbert and Susan Gubar, 153–164. Bloomington: Indiana University Press, 1979.

Kamuf, Peggy. *Fictions of Feminine Desire: Disclosures of Heloise.* Lincoln: University of Nebraska, 1982.

Keller, Lynn, and Cristanne Miller. " 'the tooth of disputation': Marianne Moore's Marriage," *Sagetrieb* 6, no. 3 (Winter 1987): 99–116.

Kenner, Hugh. "Disliking It." In *A Homemade World: The American Modernist Writers*, 91–118. New York: William Morrow and Company, 1975.

———. *The Pound Era.* Berkeley: University of California Press, 1971.

Kreymborg, Alfred, ed. *Others: An Anthology of New Verse.* New York: Alfred A. Knopf, 1917.

Kristeva, Julia. *Desire in Language*, trans. Thomas Gora, Alice Jardine, and Leon S. Roudiez. New York: Columbia University Press, 1978.

Lacan, Jacques. *Feminine Sexuality: Jacques Lacan and the école freudienne*, eds. Juliet Mitchell and Jacqueline Rose. New York: Norton, 1982.

Lipking, Lawrence. *Abandoned Women and Poetic Tradition.* Chicago: University of Chicago Press, 1988.

McConnell-Ginet, Sally, Ruth Borker, and Nelly Furman, eds. *Women and Language in Literature and Society.* New York: Praeger, 1980.

Macherey, Pierre. *A Theory of Literary Production*, trans. Geoffrey Wall. London: Routledge & Kegan Paul, 1978.

Marianne Moore Newsletter 1–7 (1977–1983). Ed. Patricia C. Willis.

Martin, Taffy. *Marianne Moore: Subversive Modernist.* Austin: University of Texas Press, 1986.

———. "Portrait of a Writing Master: Beyond the Myth of Marianne Moore." *Twentieth Century Literature* 30, nos. 2–3 (Summer-Fall 1984): 192–204.

Merrin, Jeredith. *An Enabling Humility: Marianne Moore, Elizabeth Bishop, and the Uses of Tradition*. New Brunswick: Rutgers University Press, 1990.

Miller, J. Hillis. *Poets of Reality: Six Twentieth-Century Writers*. New York: Atheneum, 1969.

Miller, Nancy K. "Emphasis Added: Plots and Plausibilities in Women's Fiction." *PLMA* 96, no. 1 (January 1981): 36–48.

Milton, John. *Complete Poems and Major Prose*, ed. Merritt Y. Hughes. Indianapolis: Odyssey Press, 1957.

Molesworth, Charles. *Marianne Moore: A Literary Life*. New York: Atheneum, 1990.

Montefiore, Jan. *Feminism and Poetry*. New York: Pandora, 1987.

Moore, Marianne. *The Collected Poems*. New York: Macmillan, 1951.

———. *The Complete Poems*. New York: Macmillan and Viking, 1981.

———. *The Complete Prose*, ed. Patricia C. Willis. New York: Viking, 1987.

———. *A Marianne Moore Reader*. New York: Viking, 1961.

———. The Marianne Moore Collection. Philadelphia: Rosenbach Museum and Library.

———. *Nevertheless*. New York: Macmillan, 1944.

———. *Observations*. New York: The Dial Press. 1924.

———. *O to Be a Dragon*. New York: Viking, 1959.

———. *The Pangolin and Other Verse*. London: The Brendin Company, 1936.

———. *Poems*. London: The Egoist Press, 1921.

———. *Predilections*. New York: Viking, 1955.

———. *Selected Poems*. New York: Macmillan, 1935.

———. *What Are Years*. New York: Macmillan, 1941.

———, trans. *The Fables of La Fontaine*. New York: Viking, 1954.

Mulvey, Laura. "Visual Pleasure and Narrative Cinema." *Screen* 16, no. 3 (Autumn 1975): 6–18.

Ortner, Sherry B., and Harriet Whitehead, eds. *Sexual Meanings: The Social Construction of Gender and Sexuality*. Cambridge: Cambridge University Press, 1981.

Ostriker, Alicia. "Marianne Moore, the Maternal Hero, and American Women's Poetry." In *Marianne Moore: The Art of a Modernist*, ed. Joseph Parisi, 49–66. Ann Arbor: UMI Research Press, 1990.

———. *Stealing the Language: The Emergence of Women's Poetry in America*. Boston: Beacon Press, 1986.

———. *Writing Like a Woman*. Ann Arbor: University of Michigan Press, 1983.

Parisi, Joseph, ed. *Marianne Moore: The Art of a Modernist*. Ann Arbor: UMI Research Press, 1990.

Peterson, Jeffrey. "Notes on the Poem(s) 'Poetry': The Ingenuity of Moore's Poetic 'Place.'" In *Marianne Moore: Woman and Poet*, ed. Patricia C. Willis, 223–241. Orono: National Poetry Foundation, 1991.

Phelan, Peggy. "Weapons and Scalpels: The Early Poetry of H. D. and Marianne Moore." In *Marianne Moore: Woman and Poet*, ed. Patricia C. Willis, 403–418. Orono: National Poetry Foundation, 1991.

Pound, Ezra. *The Cantos*. New York: New Directions, 1950.

———. *The Letters of Ezra Pound*, ed. D. D. Paige. New York: Harcourt, Brace, Jovanovich, 1950.

————. *Literary Essays of Ezra Pound*, ed. T. S. Eliot. New York: New Directions, 1935.

————. *Personae*. New York: New Directions, 1971.

————. *The Spirit of Romance*. 1910. Reprint. Norfolk, Connecticut: J. Laughlin, 1952.

————. "Three Cantos." *Poetry* 10, nos. 3–5 (1917): 113–121, 180–188, 248–254.

Quarterly Review of Literature 4, no. 2 (1948): 121–223. "Marianne Moore." Special Issue. Ed. Jose Garcia Villa.

Rainier, Yvonne. "More Kicking and Screaming from the Narrative Front/Backwater." *Wide Angle* 7, nos. 1–2 (1985): 8–12.

Rich, Adrienne. "When We Dead Awaken: Writing as Re-Vision." In *On Lies, Secrets and Silence*, 33–49. New York: W. W. Norton, 1979.

Schulman, Grace. *Marianne Moore: The Poetry of Engagement*. Chicago: University of Illinois Press, 1986.

Schweickart, Patrocinio P. "Reading Ourselves: Toward a Feminist Theory of Reading." In *Gender and Reading*, eds. Elizabeth Flynn and Patrocinio P. Schweickart, 31–62. Baltimore: The Johns Hopkins University Press, 1986.

Sielke, Sabine. "Snapshots of Marriage, Snares of Mimicry, Snarls of Motherhood: Marianne Moore and Adrienne Rich." *Sagetrieb* 6, no. 3 (Winter 1987): 79–98.

Signs 7, no. 1 (Autumn 1981). "French Feminist Theory." Special Issue.

Slatin, John. *The Savage's Romance: The Poetry of Marianne Moore*. University Park: The Pennsylvania State University Press, 1986.

————. "Something Inescapably Typical: Questions about Gender in the Late Work of Williams and Moore." *William Carlos Williams Review* 14, no. 1 (Spring 1988): 86–103.

Stapleton, Laurence. *Marianne Moore: The Poet's Advance*. Princeton: Princeton University Press, 1978.

Stein, Gertrude. *Selected Writings*, ed. Carl Van Vechten. New York: Vintage Books, 1972.

————. *The Yale Gertrude Stein*, ed. Richard Kostelantz. New Haven, Connecticut: Yale University Press, 1980.

Steinman, Lisa. "Marianne Moore: The Anaconda-Like Curves of Central Bearings." In *Made in America: Science, Technology and American Modernist Poetics*, 113–132. New Haven, Connecticut: Yale University Press, 1987.

Stevens, Wallace. "About One of Marianne Moore's Poems." In *Marianne Moore: A Collection of Critical Essays*, ed. Charles Tomlinson, 107–111. Englewood Cliffs, New Jersey: Prentice-Hall, 1969.

————. *The Collected Poems*. New York: Alfred Knopf, 1981.

————. *The Necessary Angel*. New York: Alfred A. Knopf, 1951.

Thomas, Edward. *Feminine Influence on the Poets*. New York: John Lane Company, 1911.

Todorov, Tzvetan. *The Fantastic*, trans. Richard Howard. Ithaca, New York: Cornell University Press, 1975.

Tomlinson, Charles, ed. *Marianne Moore: A Collection of Critical Essays*. Englewood Cliffs, New Jersey: Prentice-Hall, 1969.

Twentieth Century Literature 30, nos. 2–3 (Summer-Fall 1984). "Marianne Moore." Special Issue. Ed. Andrew J. Kappel.

Van Doren, Mark. "Women of Wit." *The Nation* 113, no. 2938 (26 October 1921): 481–482.

Vendler, Helen, "Marianne Moore." In *Part of Nature, Part of Us: Modern American Poets*, 59–76. Cambridge: Harvard University Press, 1980.

Vickers, Nancy J. "Diana Described: Scattered Woman and Scattered Rhyme." In *Writing and Sexual Difference*, ed. Elizabeth Abel, 95–110. Chicago: University of Chicago Press, 1982.

Walker, David. *The Transparent Lyric*. Princeton: Princeton University Press, 1984.

Williams, William Carlos. *Imaginations: Five Experimental Prose Pieces*. London: Mac-Gibbon & Kee, 1970.

————. *Selected Poems*. New York: New Directions, 1969.

Willis, Patricia C. "MM, Hardy, and Critics." *Marianne Moore Newsletter* 2, no. 2 (Fall 1978): 7–10.

————. "The Road to Paradise: First Notes on Marianne Moore's 'An Octopus.'" *Twentieth Century Literature* 30, nos. 2–3 (Summer-Fall 1984): 242–272.

Willis, Patricia C., and Clive E. Driver. "Bibliographic Numbering and Marianne Moore." *PBSA* 70 (1976): 261–263.

Wittig, Monique. "One Is Not Born a Woman." *Feminist Issues* 1, no. 2 (Winter 1981): 47–54.

————. "The Point of View: Universal or Particular." *Feminist Issues* 3, no. 2 (Fall 1983): 63–69.

Wolf, Janet. *The Social Production of Art*. London: Macmillan, 1981.

INDEX